Breaking The Script

Breaking the Script
A True Story of Finding Fame, Conquering Mental Health and the Search for Real Happiness Within

Stephanie Waring

Published by Game Changer Publishing

Paperback ISBN: 978-1-966659-52-5
Hardcover ISBN: 978-1-966659-53-2
Digital ISBN: 978-1-966659-54-9

GC GAME CHANGER PUBLISHING

www.GameChangerPublishing.com

Dedication

To Mia and Lexi, my beautiful girls, This book is a testament to the lessons I've learned, the challenges I've faced, and the dreams I've pursued, all in the hope that you will always believe in your own strength, courage and limitless potential. May you walk through life with kindness, resilience, and the knowledge that you are deeply loved.

All my love,

Mum

READ THIS FIRST

Just to say thanks for buying and reading my book—if you'd like to work with me, don't hesitate to contact me

Breaking the Script

A True Story of Finding Fame, Conquering Mental Health and the Search for Real Happiness Within

STEPHANIE WARING

Foreword

Queen Elizabeth II famously said she 'had to be seen to be believed'. I feel the same is true of Stephanie Waring. I first encountered Steph in the canteen of our then television studios, fiercely berating a fellow actor for queue-jumping and taking a bite of the last chocolate muffin before he'd paid for it. A vision in cerise couture, sleek, bobbed hair and immaculate make-up; it could have been Cindy Cunningham herself tearing a strip off the cheeky cast member. Except it wasn't. The similarities between the character and actress end in appearance. She embraced him warmly and offered to run lines for an upcoming scene of which he was nervous. This was my first glimpse into the skill and generosity of this powerhouse of illusion and talent.

Steph is a consummate professional. A special type of actor for whom one feels utterly 'safe' in crafting lines. It's the writer's job to make words leap off the page, but it's rare to hear them brought to life with the rhythm, panache and deliciousness Steph Waring can whip up. Steph is a writer's gift. She has the comedy timing of Julie Walters, or Jennifer Saunders - paired with the chameleon-like pathos and gravitas of a young Streep.

Some of the work of which I am most proud, is work performed by Steph. Her ability to say one thing with her mouth, another with her body, and portray an utterly contrary emotion with the tiniest flicker of an eye is both mesmerising and unique. Her understanding and veneration of the English language is awe-inspiring, which is why it came as no surprise to learn she can write as well as she can act.

Having enjoyed working with Steph for many years, the last 6 months have been a particular privilege. Watching any creature or human evolve is a beautiful thing to behold, but Stephanie's tenacity, work ethic, belief and hard graft have been unwavering. The journey hasn't always been easy, but I can promise, it's been authentic, important and successful. The book you are about to read cannot be simply categorised as the biography of a television star. To categorise it in any way whatsoever, would diminish some part of it, in some way. So what is it?

Personally, I feel it is an account. It is an open letter. It's a confession. It's an exorcism. It's a woman stepping into her power by tackling her perceived weaknesses one by one. It is a catalogue of errors and triumphs, of successes and failures, of judgments - both self-imposed, fictitious and external. It is a beautifully honest love letter to both oneself and the reader. Stephanie's book isn't a ten-a-penny, happy-clappy guide to self-improvement, it is a wailing banshee of a book roaring through the storm one moment, and a tranquil body of water the next. It's a practical, totally coherent and comprehensive juxtaposition of a book, rooted in hope, hilarity, faith and how to triumph over mental illness. It's about the beauty of broken porcelain becoming infinitely stronger and more valuable when repaired with pure gold and not just glue.

Waring has never been one to paper over a crack or stick a plaster on something. She rolls her sleeves up, gets to work and doesn't stop until she's gained a balanced, expert knowledge of every issue.

Perhaps, most importantly and most poignantly, it is written from her gorgeous heart in the only language Stephanie speaks: plain, simple, honest English. This is not a celebrity biography, you won't find snide barbs, whinges, grudges or exposés in here.

What you *will* find is a rare and enigmatic soul, sharing the breathtaking stories of the secret battles she lived in real time, discreetly, behind the cameras - whilst starring in one of UK's most famous award-winning dramas - without wavering, without faltering, and *critically* - without anyone realising.

If you act, perform, feel you have mental health issues, big or small, this book is for you. Though desperately and heartbreakingly hard to read at points, practically, it's the *easiest* book to read thanks to Waring's witty turn of phrase, her clear penmanship, and her set of personally created, tried-and-tested methods for dealing with any situation.

This is an incredible woman unscripted, uncensored and every word is her own - not that of a writer, not that of a manager. This is Stephanie Waring's personal manuscript - and it's a masterpiece.

I defy you to read this book and not fall in love with Steph. Furthermore, I set you the challenge: in Steph's beautiful and deeply experienced hands - fall in love with yourself.

Live the life you deserve.

– Rob Ellis
Writer / Producer

Table of Contents

INTRODUCTION

The Catalyst

Friday, 22 March 2024 – the day my life would change in a way I could never have expected. Just a month earlier, there had been an announcement that sent shockwaves through my Lime Pictures family. The television show *Hollyoaks*, a part of my life since I was 18 years old, was facing a drastic change. A huge number of job losses were expected across every department, including the cast. The soap was cutting its episodes from five to three per week, turning them into 20-minute bursts of drama that could be watched in bite-sized chunks or all three as a one-hour omnibus binge. This change was meant to align with how viewers now watch television. Many shows are streamed for ease and convenience in this fast-paced, saturated world of entertainment. I understood we had to move with the times, and I was sure Cindy Cunningham would be high-heeling her way right along with it.

Most cast members were called into meetings the previous day. I, however, was unavailable due to an appointment, so my meeting was scheduled for the next day. Throughout that afternoon, I was being drip-fed news of the characters who had been axed, and it was devastating to hear. I felt increasingly nervous about my own position – no one's job was guaranteed. But everyone kept reassuring me: 'They will not get rid of Cindy.' 'You'll be fine; you've just signed a year-long contract – of course you're safe.' 'Cindy is an original character; they'll keep the familiar faces.' 'They'll protect the originals.'

Despite all of this, I couldn't shake the unease I felt the night before. I tried to reassure myself that everything would be okay.

They say you should trust your gut. For years now, my gut has warned me of bad news before it actually arrived. Everything might seem normal on the surface, but deep down, there's an unsettled feeling that something isn't quite right. There's a reason your gut is called the second brain – it's your intuition speaking to you.

I walked into the office. There were two people there for the meeting: the newly appointed executive producer – a stalwart behind the scenes in various roles for years – and the long-standing head of production, who I'd known since I began on the show back in 1996. They asked me to sit. They explained that they'd be reading a scripted statement. As I listened, I could barely process what was being said. I was just waiting for the words I longed to hear: *'And therefore, we'd like Cindy to stay.'* But as the statement neared its close, before the final words were even spoken, I felt a tear roll down my cheek. I was shaking as I looked at the two of them.

Then it happened.

'And with that said, we will be losing Cindy from the show. I'm so sorry, Steph.'

The world stopped for a second as I replayed those words in my head.

Then... I lost my shit.

'What? No! You mean you're not taking me to the 30th?' I blurted out, referencing the upcoming anniversary of the show – a milestone that meant so much to the long-standing cast. 'I don't understand. No, I don't understand. I don't understand!'

I was frantic. 'But I've been so loyal. Please, no. This is my life. I love my job – please, no!'

Hysterically crying, I repeated myself, hoping one of them would see my distress and take it all back. Had they made a mistake? My world felt like it was imploding.

Through my tears, I demanded to know, 'How am I on that list?

Cindy is an original! I'm the longest-serving female character. I was the first person to give birth on the show.' I was clutching at anything, anything at all, to make them realise their mistake. How?

Why was I the only original being cut? I couldn't understand. It felt so cold.

I could see the distress I was causing them. I don't think they expected a reaction quite like mine. Then they said it: 'But we're not killing Cindy. You could come back.'

'What? What am I hearing? Why would they want Cindy out, just to bring her back?'

I was then told it was about numbers and the story arc.

'Numbers? I'm sorry, but Cindy is not a number – she's a fucking icon!' Now, I didn't say that last bit out loud, but I wanted to.

I wanted to scream: *It's your bloody job to create the story and protect your long-standing characters!* After 16 years and a 28-year-strong character, it should have been *my* choice to hang up her heels.

But instead, I said, 'Just tell me when I'm going.' My new contract was set to start the following month, on 27 April. I had signed it, so I presumed I'd begin it and see out the year. What followed, though, was far from what I was expecting. They told me I would be leaving in July – just 12 weeks away.

'JULY?!!!!'

I felt like I had swallowed a grenade, and it exploded inside me. A switch flipped. I couldn't make sense of it, so I fired back with all the ammunition I had, a few expletives rolling off my tongue like bullets. Yeah, I took it *really* well. They tried so hard to calm me down, to get me to breathe, but I was in full fight-or-flight mode. And after my fight, in true dramatic fashion, I fled the room.

I was still crying as I made my way through the building I had known my whole adult life, not quite grasping what had just happened. It felt like someone had died. My whole world had fallen apart in that moment. Everything I thought I knew had been taken from me so easily. I felt like nothing – like I didn't matter. Why? I'm professional. I'm well-liked – at least, I thought I was. I do a good job. *What the actual fuck.*

I ended up in makeup – I just needed to see a friendly face. There were a couple of cast members there, Kirsty Leigh Porter and Jennifer Metcalfe. Through my tears, I said, 'I'm gone. They've axed me.' From my distress, they took me in their arms and held me.

Jen led me into the makeup office so I could cry and calm down. She sat with me, trying to comfort me, listing every positive she could think of to help me see some light and come to terms with my fate.

'I need to speak to Tom,' I said, referring to my fiancé. I fumbled for my phone, barely able to see the screen through my tears, and handed it to Jen so she could pull up his name on FaceTime. She handed the phone back to me and left the room so I could talk to him in private.

When Tom answered, he was met with my tears, mascara streaking down my face as I struggled to catch my breath and tell him the awful news – I had been axed. He was in disbelief but calm, telling me to pull myself together and that he would leave work and meet me at home. At that point, I was in no state to drive. Others came into the office, trying to offer support and telling me not to drive, but I couldn't stay there any longer. I needed to be anywhere but there. I needed Tom. So I got in my car and left.

While I was driving, I received a voice message from Greg Finnegan, one of my fellow cast members who had also been cut from the show. Greg, who played James, said he couldn't believe it and was so sorry. His message made me cry even more, but it also comforted me, knowing he understood what I was going through. He had been with the show for 10 years himself.

No one could believe it. I think my axing was the most shocking of all.

I arrived home 30 minutes later to find Tom waiting for me outside. As I got out of the car, he picked me up in his arms like I was a small child needing a parent. He held me while I sobbed and sobbed, repeating to him everything that had just happened. I knew it – something in my gut had been telling me this was going to happen, and now it had.

Then, as if the day couldn't get any worse, more bad news came that afternoon. A press release announced that 20 cast members would vanish from *Hollyoaks* in September as the show planned to flash forward an entire year. This meant that those of us leaving in July wouldn't even get an exit from the show. Cindy wouldn't get to say goodbye? It was devastating. My thoughts turned to the fans – the ones who had been on this journey with me, who had invested in these much-loved characters. They wouldn't get any closure.

But then, I found out that Cindy *would* get her exit after all. A few others, including James and Ellis Hollis – who played my little brother Tom – would also get their goodbyes. Ellis had been in his role since he was four years old, giving 20 years of his life to the show. Cindy and Tom would leave together, fleeing to Spain to start a new life.

This is where listening to your gut is so important. My manager, Melanie, called me. This woman is an absolute warrior in the business – she can pretty much get you whatever you want. No one says no to Melanie. She couldn't believe the news herself and was immediately on the phone, trying to find out why. I hadn't asked her to do this, and I had no idea what conversations she was having. All I knew was that she was trying to get them to reverse their decision.

But when she told me that, something in my gut said, *No, Melanie. I don't want it.*

PART ONE

Planting the Weeds

CHAPTER 1

Dying to Be Thin

There's never been more truth in the saying, 'Blink and you'll miss it' – a sentence I heard countless times growing up. I've lived through three full decades and am now halfway through my fourth – have I been asleep? Where did all that time go? What the hell have I been wasting my time on? The endless pursuit of the perfect body?

To others, I might already be there – I've always been there – but to me, no matter how in shape I am, no matter how low that number on the scale goes, I'm just not skinny enough. Not good enough. Not sexy enough. Not pretty enough. My cellulite is so bad. 'I'll be happy when I have no cellulite.' My days were consumed by this warped sense of how I look to others, but it's only *me* who chastises and criticises. It's me who batters and bruises myself with self-doubt, fuelled by the relentless noise in my head.

Sometimes, that noise is amplified by trolls on the internet – anonymous voices hiding behind the safety of their screens, pointing out if I've gained a pound or two. During my time on *Dancing on Ice*, they went hard: 'Her thighs are *sooooo* big', 'She's tiny, but whoa, look at them fat legs', 'She's so out of proportion.'

And then, if I was photographed at an event or papped outside a restaurant, it was almost guaranteed to end up in the *Daily Mail*. The articles were either rehashes of past events from my life, made-up nonsense about my love life, or over-the-top, gushing pieces about how fabulous I supposedly looked. Those would make me want to throw up in my mouth. Reading about myself through someone else's eyes was a surreal, grotesque experience.

But the worst part? The comments. Oh, the comments. Every ounce of my being would scream, 'DON'T LOOK AT THE COMMENTS,' but I'd still scroll down.

I don't know if these so-called trolls get paid to tear people down or if they even know who the person in the article is, but they go in. Hard.

'She's so skinny.'

'Her face is frozen.' (Still not sure how you can move your face in a photograph.)

'She looks like a lollipop head.'

'That girl needs to eat a burger.'

'She's so scrawny.'

'She's so overrated.'

'Daily Mail, stop trying to make Steph Waring happen.'

That last one always made me laugh, as if I had any control over what was being written about me.

And while I knew the skinny comments were insults, I liked them. They reaffirmed and validated what my inner child learned all those years ago – the weeds I planted: *You will be loved when you are thin.*

Forty-six years of life, and I'm still trying to navigate the spaghetti-like entanglement of beliefs ingrained in me since childhood. Beliefs that have imprisoned me, inhibited me. For far too long, I've played the best role of my life: The Victim.

I vaguely remember a time when I was free. Free of thought. Free of that other voice that lives in your head – the one you find yourself constantly arguing with. The judge. The biggest critic. The voice that holds you back and tells you that you're not good enough, not worthy enough.

When I was a baby, I knew no fear. I knew no future or past. I was whole and present.

As a toddler, my free spirit began to explore the world, captivated by my surroundings, using my senses, experiencing complete joy, fully aware.

Then we're taught how to communicate – by our parents, by those around us. Rules are put in place. We're told when we're bad and when we're good. When we're bad, we're chastised, often by a big, scary, loud grown-up voice. Back in my day, a 'good hiding' was always on the cards. We learned fear. We learned there were consequences if what we did wasn't deemed acceptable by the adults.

When we were good, we were praised and rewarded. And so, we learned that to be accepted, we must please others.

That's where the people-pleasing part of my personality was born.

As I grew up and entered the world of school, mixing with other children, I quickly began to shift from the free-spirited toddler I once was. I started learning behaviours and emotions through my ego. Other children didn't like me. Why? Because I was fat and uninteresting – or so I told myself. I was never a naughty child; I can't remember ever misbehaving or doing anything that would warrant a good telling-off. The only explanation my mind could come up with was: *I am not worthy because I am fat.* Others told me I was, so it had to be true.

Even now, just writing that sentence down, I know how extremely false it is. Being a little overweight as a child is not WHO I AM. But, nonetheless, that core belief stuck with me for many years. Even today, it lingers. It's not as strong as it once was, but it's still there.

How does a child get to the point of nearly dying because they are so desperate for love, unable to recognise the love that has always surrounded them? How does a child stop eating because they think being thin will bring them the love and adoration they crave? That child was me.

Years of feeling like I fell short – not being good enough for my friends, my family, or that boy I desperately wanted to fancy me – shaped me. Don't get me wrong; I had the personality. I was fun, imaginative, and full of laughter. I wanted to be an actress. But I tied my self-worth as a teenager to my appearance. I believed being beautiful and loved meant being thin. Fat, to me, was my biggest enemy. One day, I decided, *That's it. I'm going on a diet.*

The diet had no endpoint.

In some ways, I think the diet has lasted 30 years.

It started slowly. I never skipped meals; I just cut out the junk. The endless biscuits I'd devour while watching TV? Gone. The second or third bowl of cereal? Reduced to just one (a large one, of course).

I began moving more, exercising, and walking. I didn't know what carbs or protein were – back then, the internet didn't exist. All the information constantly shoved down our throats today wasn't a thing. All I knew was that fat was bad. So, I cut out the fat.

My body started to change, slowly but surely. And with that change came attention – not just from my friends, but from boys. The feeling I got when someone said, 'Have you lost weight?' was indescribable. Even now, if someone says it, that old feeling washes over me. Though now, my negative adult brain chimes in with, *Did you think I was fat before?*

Over the course of a year, my body shrank. I discovered ways to eat more while reducing calories. But I became afraid to eat the foods I used to enjoy, fearing I'd put the weight back on. I increased my daily exercising to three times a day. My favourite workout videos back then were Cindy Crawford and Cher.

Every morning, I'd run up and down the stairs for a count of 100, making sure I didn't miss a single step. If I deviated from my routine, I'd panic. I weighed myself every day.

I was deep in something I didn't fully understand.

One day, a teacher pulled me aside after class. They suggested I see a doctor because they were worried about my weight loss. At the time, I think I'd gone from around 132 lbs to just over 100. At 5 ft 1 and 13 years old, I wasn't *too* skinny – I was perfectly slim.

Can you imagine how it felt to be told by someone of importance, like a teacher, that they were worried about me because they thought I was too thin?

I felt ecstatic.

I can still remember how it went when I went to the doctor. I sat down and explained that my teacher had told me to come because of my weight loss. At the time, I didn't understand what the big deal was. All I knew was that someone cared, and my weight loss was the reason why.

The doctor asked me to step on the scale. I was nervous because I'd eaten lunch, hadn't emptied my bladder, and was fully clothed – this was not my usual morning ritual. Still, I stepped on, and the dial jumped to 47 kg (about 104 lbs).

She told me to sit down and promptly informed me there was nothing wrong with me. She said I was around the same weight as her and that I was at a perfectly healthy weight, then sent me on my way.

I was crushed. How could she compare my 13-year-old body to her middle-aged, 40-something self? She didn't care – at least, that's what I thought. Something inside me needed to be *not okay* to validate myself, to prove her wrong.

I don't know why I wanted something to be wrong with me. Maybe it was the feeling of being noticed, of being seen, even if that meant wearing the victim label. So, I cut out more food. And then more. And more.

Over the next few months, I rapidly wasted away. Everyone noticed, but not in the way I'd imagined. I didn't gain loads of friends or acceptance. Instead, the opposite happened. No one stuck around. I had no friends. I was a shadow of my former self. My personality was nonexistent.

Schoolwork became my focus, along with my diet and exercise. That was all I had.

It all came to a head one day when I fainted at school and was taken to the nurse's office. My mum came to pick me up, and I could tell she'd been crying. My dad pulled me out of school and took me to the doctor – a different one this time.

This doctor confirmed what I already suspected: I had anorexia nervosa. Finally, a label, I thought. Finally, someone was acknowledging that something was wrong with me.

The doctor gave me a diet sheet to follow and sent me on my way again. At that point, I went to live with my dad. When I was younger, I'd put him on a pedestal, so I chose to stay with him while I was off school, hoping to get better on my own.

I failed.

I was fully in the grip of a mental illness that was killing me. And even though I knew it was killing me, I was powerless to stop it. It got to the point where I was scared to drink a can of Diet Coke because it had *one calorie*.

I had barely turned 15 when my next doctor's visit became a very serious one. I remember her words clearly: 'Stephanie, you may as well go and get run over by a bus because you're going to die any day now.'

I weighed 52 lbs. I'm not sure the NHS would approve of this approach today, but I was promptly admitted into the Adolescent Unit of Prestwich Hospital.

CHAPTER 2

The Lost Summer

*I*t was the summer of 1993, and I spent it in a room. If you ever want to truly appreciate the smell of fresh grass – or fresh air in general – get yourself committed.

I arrived at the unit with my mum. We were shown around by a nurse named Gemma. She was bubbly and friendly, with short, bobbed blonde hair. I immediately felt a sense of ease around her. I didn't know what to expect when I was admitted here. I thought the unit was primarily for treating eating disorders, so I was shocked to discover I was the only anorexic kid there – apart from one other girl who had bulimia.

As I walked through the unit, it became clear that the other children came from completely different walks of life, each with their own serious mental health problems – things I'd never encountered in my sheltered 15 years. While the other kids in the unit lived in dormitories, I was given my own room. I was told that, under no circumstances, was I allowed to leave it except to use the bathroom and attend the morning meetings in the day room.

I had a target: to gain 49 lbs in about two months. The longer it took me to put on the weight, the longer I had to stay in that room. The room itself was sparse – just a bed with one of those uncomfortable hospital mattresses, a single wardrobe, and a dresser. My mum tried to make it bearable by kitting it out with a TV (back then, we only had four channels and an indoor aerial that I had to constantly adjust for a decent picture), a stereo, and my Sega Mega Drive. I could only play one game on it: *Sonic the Hedgehog*. As you can imagine, I got pretty good at it.

Before my mum left, the head of the unit came in to talk to us about what was expected of me. I had to gain three pounds per week until I hit my target. If I didn't, there would be consequences. Never wanting to disappoint or fail, I was terrified – because even though I was starving, I wasn't sure I could do it.

He laid out my meal plan, and it was overwhelming, to say the least:

Breakfast
- 2 Weetabix with gold-top milk
- 2 rounds of toast

11 a.m.
- 2 biscuits
- Half a pint of gold-top milk

Lunch
- A full dinner and a pudding

3 p.m.
- Sandwich
- Half a pint of gold-top milk

Dinner
- Another full meal with pudding

9 p.m.

- 2 slices of toast
- Half a pint of gold-top milk

That's a lot of food – around 3,000 calories a day. I had only *dreamt* of eating so much. Some people think anorexics aren't hungry. That couldn't be further from the truth. Food was all I could think about. I dreamt about it. It consumed me. Can you imagine the damage done to children when they grow up with such deeply disturbed, learned behaviours around food?

After my mum left, I was alone. I unpacked and tried to settle in. A knock on my door signalled my first meal had arrived. It was egg and chips – the holy grail of foods. I can still remember exactly how those chips tasted; they were cooked to absolute perfection.

I sat down on my bed with the tray in front of me. It took me a while to even take a bite. I wanted to devour the plate, but guilt stopped me. I thought, *If I eat this entire plate of food, they'll think nothing is wrong with me.* That was my primary thought: *What will they think of me?*

I truly believed I would see the fat from the food instantly spread across my body. Even though my bones poked through my skin – I had to wear padding on my coccyx because the bone had broken through the skin – I couldn't shake the fear.

I ate the food, but I left a couple of chips to show them I wasn't a complete fraud. Afterwards, I frantically started doing jumping jacks and leg lifts, hoping to burn away the calories I had just eaten.

I felt dirty.

A couple of hours later, supper arrived, brought to me by one of the girls, Lisa. She was 14. She put my toast down with the glass of milk and asked me about myself. All I remember thinking was, *God, I hate milk.* I asked Lisa why she had been admitted. She was very open about why she was an inpatient: Her uncle had sexually abused her for several years – so much so, she needed a catheter. My heart broke for her.

Over the course of my first week, I met all the other kids on the unit – kids around my age, each with very different problems. These ranged from drug abuse to schizophrenia, some illnesses I didn't understand at all and, frankly, didn't want to understand or dive into. I just got to know these kids as kids.

A week went by, and it was time for my first weigh-in. I was so nervous to see the scale go up. However, to my shock and surprise, I had lost a pound. How? I was so confused. I had pretty much polished off all the meals I'd been given. Apparently, this was the kickstart my 15-year-old metabolism needed after being in starvation mode for the better part of two years. Bewildered, I went back to my room.

Shortly after my weigh-in, the head of the unit came to see me to talk about my weight loss. He asked if I had been eating all my food. He asked if I had been making myself sick. The answers I gave were the truth: Yes, I had been eating my food, and no, I had never once made myself sick. I'm not sure he believed me. He was following the science, after all. If I had eaten 3,000 calories a day, I *should* have gained at least three pounds. To lose weight? He couldn't understand it, so he assumed I was lying.

It's so frustrating when you know you're telling the truth.

Putting it simply, he told me that under no circumstances would I be allowed to leave my room if I didn't put on the weight that was expected of me. He said I was only delaying the inevitable. So, I thought, *Okay, I'm going to put on the weight – even if it kills me.* This wasn't fixing my brain; it was simply my way out.

I asked my grandma to bring me some extra food when she visited. Under my bed, I had a stash of Weetabix and a packet of digestive biscuits. I just supplemented what they were giving me to eat with my secret stash.

When you're 15 years old – a child – how are you meant to understand what the hell is happening to you? I didn't even know I'd had a shitty childhood until the psychiatrist I saw weekly at the unit urged me to pick apart all 15 years of my life. The thing is, I *didn't* have a shitty childhood. I had a wonderful upbringing. But there was this belief that something other than wanting to be slim had to be the cause of the anorexia.

The psychiatrist pinned it all on significant life changes, with a salient one being my parents' divorce.

The day my dad sat my sister and me down to tell us our family was splitting up was, at that point, the worst day of my life. I was nine years old. I can still recall the moment, like a scene from a movie stuck on repeat. We were heartbroken. To stop the tears, my dad promptly followed the news with, 'Fancy a Chinese?'

I took comfort from food. Mum and Dad were divorcing, but man, that was a good special fried rice.

It wasn't just my parents' divorce the psychiatrist had her eyes on. As soon as I mentioned the dynamics of my relationship with my sister Rachel, she was all over it like a rash, reminiscing about one Christmas when our parents got us a pool table. It wasn't a huge, full-size one, but it was perfect for us. I played against my wayward sister – who would sometimes beat the shit out of me if I so much as looked at her sideways. Because I won a game, I dared to tease her. Big mistake. She promptly smashed the cue over my head, breaking it in half. Needless to say, we never played pool again. And this story prompted the ever-so-repetitive phrase, 'Tell me more,' from the psychiatrist.

Rachel was the first person in my life I had a bond with, apart from my parents. She's two and a half years older than me and has always been against the rules. Since she was a toddler, she didn't give a flying fuck –

she just did what she wanted, took what she wanted, and if anyone got in her way, they'd know about it.

One of my earliest memories of Rachel being in trouble was when I was around three years old. We lived in our first house as a family. My dad was pretending to be on the phone with the police because Rachel had been bad, and all I could hear was him saying the police were coming to take her away. I remember her crying so hard, and I was crying too because I didn't want her to be sent away.

That was the first time I think I felt the fear of abandonment. And throughout my whole life, I've done anything to keep the peace – even to my own detriment. I was, and always have been, a sensitive soul. The people pleaser. The fixer.

Rachel was never out of trouble, mainly for stealing money and skipping school. The worst punishment was when she got the belt. I could hear her yelps as it thrashed against her bottom or legs, and all I felt was helplessness and anxiety, just wishing the screams would stop.

This was the '80s, when that kind of punishment was deemed acceptable. Personally, I never got the belt, but I did get a good hiding from time to time. That's just how it was back then.

Most of my punishments were for teasing Rachel or winding her up. We were sisters – it's what we did. But her reactions usually left me with a dead arm or my records smashed in half. (To anyone born post-2000 who doesn't know what records are, google it.)

Rachel and I were – and still are – complete opposites. She was a tomboy, hanging out with boys, riding BMX bikes, and spending all day outside getting up to God knows what. She was also very athletic and competed in gymnastics.

I, on the other hand, was not athletic. The most exercise I got was lifting biscuits out of the biscuit tin. I tried gymnastics too, but I struggled. I rarely made it over the vault.

I was a Barbie girl. I loved my dolls and could play with them all day long. I was very imaginative, always creating other worlds for myself and playing make-believe. I was girly to my core, fully bought into every Disney film narrative about the prince saving the princess. Honestly, I blame Disney for a lot of my issues.

Rachel was expelled from three schools during her teenage years. The first, she lasted less than a year. The second was because she just never showed up. And the third? That was when she went to live with my dad in his newly built pub.

On her first day at the new school, Dad told her under no circumstances should she do anything to get into trouble. Cut to her stealing two bottles of vodka from the pub and getting a couple of students so paralytic they ended up in the hospital. She lasted *one day* before being sent back to live with Mum and me.

I don't know how my mum coped. Back then, there were no mobile phones to track your location – just your word that you'd be home on time.

Mum would often get a knock on the door from the police, bringing Rachel home.

God, I wish I had my mum's strength. If one of my girls ever did this to me, I don't know if I could survive the anxiety.

At 15 years old, Rachel didn't bother with school anymore. She left and never looked back. She ended up having a baby at 16 – my niece, Terri, who is now 31 (okay, now I feel old). Her pregnancy was around the time my anorexia battle began.

I was always on some sort of diet. I'd say as young as 10, when I no longer had my mum cooking for me because I chose to live with my dad. That meant I was left to make my own food, which usually consisted of a bowl of cereal after school, a pot noodle sandwich, or a Lean Cuisine ready meal. I would read magazine articles on how to get slim legs in 28 days –

usually with a model in a bikini holding a tape measure around her waist – and study the calorie lists plastered all over the pages. But none of it ever lasted. I was too young to have the knowledge, the know-how, or the discipline it takes to lose weight.

When I was 12 and living back with my mum, I finally decided enough was enough. I was going to lose weight. My New Year's resolution was to stick to my diet until I looked good in a pair of hot pants. That was it. I polished off the remaining Cadbury Roses from the large tin and didn't look back.

* * *

Before I ended up at the unit for treatment, my relationship with Rachel started to shift. She softened. She was becoming a mother, and all her instincts to protect kicked in – including protecting me. To this day, she's my ride or die. We're still worlds apart in how we live our lives and who we are as people, but Rachel is the one person I go to when I need help or advice. She tells me the truth, and she gets me. She looked after me when I was unwell, and I'll never forget that.

I know she's proud of me for what I've achieved and what I've done with my life. My sister was never the root cause of any of my problems. Whatever happened between us when we were kids wasn't personal – we were kids; we didn't know any better. If I took an insult from her calling me fat as truth, that's on me. I made that agreement with myself – and with every other person who bullied me or called me names.

Maybe it was not having many friends in primary school that led to the inevitable, 'Well, you must have been bullied then?' It was a lie that became a truth.

The best friend, who was gorgeous and thin, stole my first-ever boyfriend's heart.

But the reality is, highlighting these events didn't cure the anorexia. It only exacerbated it. It became something bigger than it was – the ultimate victim's label. *This happened to me, therefore, I will wear it as a badge for all to see.* The thinner I got, the more sympathy I'd receive because I was broken, I was small, I was fragile.

But I was also alone. Almost invisible.

My early memories of friendships – or the lack thereof – go back to primary school. I wasn't a complete loner, but I definitely wasn't popular. I'd often play alone at break times or sit on the steps, watching the other kids and desperately hoping to be asked to join in. I rarely was.

The closest I came to feeling visible was when I was ten and planning a birthday party. At the time, I was living with my dad above my grandparents' record shop, Waring's. I loved it there. I could listen to any music I wanted, and my grandma, whom I called by her first name, Eileen, would record all my favourite albums and singles onto cassette tapes.

For my party, I invited all the popular kids and some of my actual friends. To my amazement, the most popular girl, Emma, said she would come – and so did all her friends. It was a sleepover. She even helped me plan it.

I was ecstatic.

We had the full works: disco lights, party food, pizza, sweets, all the music I could wish for, and the place to ourselves because my dad was at the pub across the road.

The night arrived, and I was so excited, watching the clock and waiting for everyone to show up. Time ticked on. A couple of my real friends arrived, but soon it dawned on me – I'd been played. Emma and her sheep didn't turn up.

I was crushed.

It was the cruellest joke, and it's a memory that has stuck with me to this day.

But we still had fun. We ate junk, danced, watched movies, and the three of us stayed up all night. The mean girls were never invited to another party again.

* * *

Secondary school was a very different experience for me. One of the popular girls from primary – let's call her 'Lucy' – was going to the same all-girls school as me. She asked if I wanted to get the bus with her. I immediately said yes and couldn't believe she wanted to be friends with me. From that first bus ride, we became inseparable. But also, that first bus ride was when I saw *him* – the boy who made my stomach flip. More on that later.

Lucy and I ended up in the same class and sat next to each other in most lessons. We were inseparable and, to my surprise, very popular. We were disruptive in class and pretty much did what we wanted – within reason. Like I've said, I was never a bad kid, but after years of feeling invisible and being told I was overweight for my age, I finally had a best friend. A friend who wasn't just gorgeous but wanted to be best friends with *me*.

After school, we'd run home and call each other straight away. I still remember her landline number. Most nights, we'd meet and hang out at the park or have sleepovers. The first time I tried alcohol was with Lucy– two cans of Kestrel Super Strength. I got so drunk I couldn't stand up, but all I remember was laughing. Laughing so hard I nearly peed.

I did envy Lucy. I thought she was beautiful. She was small like me in height, but unlike me, she had the most amazing figure – petite with massive boobs. I, on the other hand, was still convinced I was overweight for my age. Not hugely overweight, but on the bigger side of slim.

Looking back now, I was just healthy. I wasn't overweight in any way. But it was the constant reminders from others that made me believe I was. The one person I thought would never use my size against me was Lucy. But I was wrong. She would often 'playfully' call me names – *fat fingers* being one of her terms of endearment. She even wrote that in a birthday card. *'Happy Birthday Fat Fingers!'*

However, the worst thing she ever did – the cruellest joke I've ever experienced – is something I haven't, and will never, forget.

Since I was little, I've always wanted to be an actress. It was all I dreamt about and talked about. I joined Oldham Theatre Workshop, where I stayed for a year. Then Lucy joined too. Deep down, I knew she only wanted to join because I was there. I liked having something that was just mine.

One day, I received a letter in the post. The address on the envelope was spelled wrong, but at the time, that didn't mean anything to me. I opened the letter, and it was supposedly from David Johnson – the teacher who ran Oldham Theatre Workshop and was responsible for launching the careers of many famous names from the north of Manchester.

The letter said Disney was casting a film and looking for young actors who were, to put it bluntly, fat. The wording wasn't quite so harsh, but that was the gist. As I read it, it all sounded so convincing. It mentioned flying to America, staying at the Hilton Hotel, going to Buena Vista Studios – it included a full itinerary.

Everything about it sounded legit.

I remember being so excited, showing my mum, and thinking, *I've been picked! I'm going to be in a Disney film!* The feeling was like no other. I didn't even care that it was because of my size.

But as I re-read the letter over and over, my gut kicked in. Something wasn't quite right. I noticed David's signature didn't match the one on the official paperwork I had from the workshop. Then there was my address – how it was spelled – and the handwriting. It all felt too familiar.

The week before I received the letter, Lucy had mentioned helping her sister out in her office, where she had access to a typewriter. At the time, this was just a suspicion. So, I took the letter to the workshop. After class, I pulled David to one side and showed it to him.

He confirmed what I already knew.

It wasn't real. It was a prank.

A cruel fucking prank.

I told Lucy, but I never accused her. Something inside me didn't want to lose her friendship, even though I knew what she had done. What does that say about me? Once again, I didn't know my own worth. I gave this girl my power and let her walk all over me, and it didn't stop there.

When I decided to go on my diet, it took until around July 1992 for the changes in my body to become really noticeable. At that point, I was eating pretty much the same thing every day at school – beans on toast. And guess what? Lucy would eat exactly the same thing, but she would always leave a mouthful on her plate. I found this very bizarre, like it was some kind of food competition – who could eat the least.

I would always finish my food. Mealtimes were an event for me as I became more and more restrictive. Lucy didn't need to lose any weight, but as I lost mine and my face began to shine through, I realised I was pretty. I had a beautiful face hidden under those chubby cheeks.

Jealousy was rife.

I didn't know it at the time. I was oblivious to the fact that my best friend, someone I thought the world of, could actually be jealous of me. What did I have? I wasn't even aware of what a fucking amazing human I was. I was funny, entertaining, the class clown, kind, and generous. I was still that sensitive little girl desperate to be liked and accepted.

As my disease started to take hold in the months that followed, I began to waste away before everyone's eyes. Slowly, my friends – including Lucy, who was the first to go, taking most people with her – began to distance themselves from me.

Nobody understood what was happening to me.

Even I didn't understand.

I knew what anorexia was – I even wished for it. You could say I manifested it. I was 10 years old at the time, and if you grew up in the '90s, you might remember the ITV show *Children's Ward*. There was a storyline about a girl with anorexia. I didn't know what that meant; I just knew if you had it, you were skinny. So, I wished for it.

That old saying 'Be careful what you wish for' has never been more true.

I did have one friend who stuck around – Lisa. We're still friends to this day. She's responsible for every hair creation that's graced every red carpet event I've been to.

By the time I was hospitalised, I had nothing but my disease controlling me. As I continued to restrict my food, the pounds kept falling away. I was nothing but bones. My skin turned yellow because my liver was failing. My hair became thin and brittle. My body was coated in a fine, downy hair – my own body's survival mechanism kicking in to keep me warm.

The thought of food consumed me. I would feed everyone around me and take pleasure in watching others gorge on food I could only dream about. I became obsessive about my surroundings. Nothing could be out of place. I poured everything into my schoolwork. The dream of becoming an actress slowly faded. I even turned down my first audition because I was too ill and weak.

So, what was it?

I would sit in that small room across from a stranger once a week, talking about my life. They would listen, but I don't remember them ever giving me the tools to unwind the core beliefs I'd made with myself.

I still have some fears.

It's taken a long time – a lot of work, mindset shifts, and tools I've learned – but I'm slowly taking back control. I'm finally unwiring the agreements I made with myself as a child. I'm removing those weeds and replacing them with new, positive seeds.

But it's taken 30 years.

I'm writing this book in the hope that if someone reads it and is suffering the way I did, I can help them. I want to stop them from wasting precious years of their lives fearing themselves and letting other people's opinions shape their core beliefs.

Because what other people think about us? That's none of our business.

It's just an opinion, their point of view. It doesn't make it fact.

It only becomes truth if we agree with them.

I tell my children all the time: Anything negative that comes their way from others is not truth. The way others see the world is not how we see it. Everyone's perception is different. The bully who called me fat? That was their opinion. My friend who thought I was beautiful? Their opinion.

Which one you take on as your truth is up to you.

Four months of my life spent institutionalised – the whole summer of 1993. For two of those months, all I had was that tiny room, which I made my home. That's how long it took me to gain 42 lbs in weight. The target was 98 lbs, the lowest they would consider acceptable, given my age and height.

When I finally gave in and started gaining the weight, it wasn't because I wanted to get better. It was just a means to an end: to get the hell out of that room. Once I hit my goal, I'd be allowed to move into the dormitory with the other girls. I'd be allowed to go to the school they had there and even join the weekly day trips out.

The weekends were the loneliest. Most of the other kids went home to their parents or caregivers. It was just me and the girl with bulimia, staying full-time, who were only allowed family visitation. It was brutal.

But I do have some fond memories. I'd been so sheltered my whole life, and meeting and living with a group of kids from all walks of life, all with different and unique problems, was eye-opening. I felt like I was in a television drama, watching from the sidelines.

I got to know the other kids really well, and they were all so lovely to me. I remember one night when the girls sneaked me out of my room. I hid under a bed in the dorm while the nurse did her rounds. Of course, I got caught and sent back to where I belonged, but the thrill of being a little naughty got my adrenaline pumping.

I listened to their stories about what had happened to them. They were so open with me, and to them, I wasn't a freak. They affectionately nicknamed me 'The Cindy Crawford of the unit', which, let me tell you, was quite the compliment.

So, after eating – and loving every bite of it – I finally reached my goal weight. The first thing I did? I grabbed my Walkman and headphones, popped in my *Michael Jackson Thriller* cassette, and took my first breath of fresh air outside. It was a sunny day, and – clich'd as it sounds – I could smell the grass. I sat down, picked at the blades of grass with my fingers, and let 'Billie Jean' blast into my ears.

I'll never forget that day or that feeling.

Although, over the years, I've definitely forgotten to appreciate being alive, being healthy, and getting to smell the grass whenever I want.

Moving into the dorms was fun. I felt like part of an exclusive group. The girls and I were so tight, and even the boys were my friends – well, apart from the one who used to stand in the corner laughing while he pissed in a plant pot.

I started at the school when term began in September, and I loved it. I wrote a lot of poems, and art quickly became my thing. I'd paint and draw most days.

Over the months, people would leave. It was always sad to say goodbye, knowing I'd probably never see them again.

One day, the unit had a new arrival – another anorexic girl moving into my old room. I was shocked when I saw her. She was so frail and gaunt, just like I had been. She was taller than me, so to me, she looked even thinner than I ever was.

Gemma, my nurse, asked if I wouldn't mind chatting with her, since she was terrified. I went in, sat with her, and she told me how beautiful I looked. I told her it was all going to be okay.

But was it?

After another two months in the unit, my weight was stable, and I had convinced the psychiatrist I was cured. I was discharged and had my own sad goodbye to the friends I'd made. We all promised to keep in touch, but unfortunately, that didn't happen. I really hope those kids who were part of my interrupted adolescence have found peace and gone on to do something amazing with their lives.

In 2005, I wrote a drama based on my time in the unit. Each episode would focus on one of the kids' journeys – how they ended up being committed and what life was like on the unit for these teens. Over the years, I've had some interest from production companies, filling me with false hope for my amazing idea. Maybe one day I'll get it made. I hope so. It's a story worth telling.

After I left the unit, it took only a month for me to drop 28 lbs of the weight I had put on. Of course, I wasn't better – too much damage had been done, and I still had no clue what the 'event' was that had stopped me from eating in the first place.

Looking back now, I think it was just fear. Fear that, in order to be loved, you had to be beautiful. I didn't know back then that people fall in love with your personality, with who you are at your core. No wonder I didn't have any friends when I was just a shell of myself – not only physically, but emotionally too. The person I was inside had become so small, she didn't have a voice anymore. I had lost who I was.

For a while, my weight hovered around 70 lbs. Eventually, I decided to try to gain weight. I didn't want a life of being in and out of institutions. I followed a diet that gave me a little more freedom, and slowly but surely, I managed to gain 14 lbs. It was barely noticeable, but I looked so much better – even though I was still tiny.

My weight stabilised at 84 lbs for a good two years.

I didn't know then that another, much bigger monster was about to enter my life – and stick around for 25 years.

PART TWO

Lights! Camera! Action!

CHAPTER 3

From Famine to Feast to Fame.

I've said before that it was always my dream to be an actress. I remember the first time I knew this – I was around four years old. I said to my mum, 'Mummy, I want to be on television one day.'

I loved watching movies. As a child, I was a huge *Star Wars* and *Superman* fan and would watch them over and over again with my dad. As I got older, I became hooked on the Australian TV shows *Neighbours* and *Home and Away*, staples of my everyday life after school. That's when my obsession with Kylie Minogue – or Charlene, as she was then – began.

I loved everything about her. Scott and Charlene were *huge* back then. I'll never forget when they got married on *Neighbours*. We even had the TV brought into the classroom for the lunchtime showing. I was nine years old, and over 20 million people tuned in to watch that episode in 1988.

Kylie had already released 'I Should Be So Lucky', and as soon as I heard it and saw the music video, I was obsessed. She was everything I wanted to be. When her first album dropped, I played it nonstop, on repeat. I knew every lyric and every dance move. In my head, I *was* Kylie – I was just a bit fatter.

Kylie exploded onto the scene in the late '80s, a product of the Stock Aitken and Waterman machine. But there was nothing manufactured about her – she just *had it*. And she still has it, with a career spanning 30+ years. She still has my heart.

No single part of the walls of the tiny box that was my room was visible: Everything was covered in Kylie posters and clippings. I still have the box of memorabilia – filled with all those clippings and posters. I found it in the loft just before I started writing this book, and it blows my mind that I kept it all these years.

I devoured every single magazine that came out, searching for anything about Kylie. I joined her fan club, and my dad took me to my first-ever concert at Birmingham NEC to see her perform.

The next concert I went to was at the Apollo in Manchester in 1990, during her *Let's Get To It* tour. This was her sexy phase when she was dating Michael Hutchence from INXS. You could see her evolving, growing up right in front of our eyes – and boy, did she own it. Kylie oozed sex appeal, and I was here for it.

At that concert, I was in the front row. I got so close to the stage that she touched my hand. As you can imagine, it was the best night of my life.

To me, Kylie was tiny and perfect. I idolised her. I even wrote to *Jim'll Fix It*, the BBC show where people wrote in to ask Jim to make their dreams come true. I wrote several times, asking if he could arrange a meeting with Kylie. Thankfully, that never transpired – otherwise, this would be a completely different book.

Okay, so I wasn't a crazy fan stalker or anything. I just loved her and her music, no matter the phase. Even when she dabbled in indie alternative music, I embraced it – or, well, I forced myself to embrace it. I'm a pop girl through and through, so thank God she threw on those gold hot pants and spun us all around with her 2000 comeback single, 'Spinning Around.'

Kylie had a lot to do with my childhood dream of being famous. I wanted the adoration, to be loved by millions, just like she was. Since I couldn't sing, I thought the next best thing was to be an actress.

When I was 12, I begged my mum to let me join Oldham Theatre Workshop, where so much northern homegrown talent started out. Most of the *Coronation Street* stars had gone there, so I applied – and I got in.

I wasn't a particularly confident child and had low self-esteem because of my weight, but I did my best to watch and learn from the others around me. At the time, one of my classmates was Suranne Jones, though back then, I knew her as Sarah. Years later, when she was in *Corrie* and I was in *Hollyoaks*, she came up to me in the Press Club in Manchester and said, 'Hi Steph, do you remember me?'

I was confused because I only saw her as Karen McDonald from *Coronation Street*. Then she said, 'It's Sarah from Oldham Theatre Workshop. We were in the same class.'

How did I not recognise her? But more to the point, I couldn't believe she remembered me all those years later. I thought I was a nobody back then.

* * *

Before my anorexia kicked in, I performed in a couple of shows with Oldham – one panto and one summer show. The panto was *Jack and the Beanstalk*, starring Anna Friel and Antony Cotton (who's spent decades now on *Corrie*). I was just a village girl. I remember my mum had to make my costume. Looking back, I think, *Bloody hell, she did a lot for me.* Driving me to Oldham, waiting in the car while I did my classes, making costumes – if my kids asked me to make a costume today, I'd promptly look online for next-day delivery.

Anyway, Antony – I adored him. I had a crush, though he had no idea I existed, and I had no idea he'd never, ever be my type. My gaydar wasn't great back then.

The summer show I did was *Worzel Gummidge*. Antony had the lead role, and this time, I had a couple of lines. Alongside me in the show was Lisa Riley, who later played Mandy Dingle in *Emmerdale*.

That summer, I started losing weight because I'd begun dieting in January of that year, 1992. Sadly, that was the last show I ever did with Oldham. As the grips of anorexia tightened, I became too weak and void of personality. I lost all my ambition to become an actress and turned my attention elsewhere.

* * *

I decided I wanted to move to France, learn the language, and work on my Grandad Jack's boat. Jack had a place in the South of France, and this became the plan.

After leaving school with good GCSEs – thank God for anorexia making me studious – I ended up going to business college instead to study business studies. I thought that was what I was meant to do, and then I'd move to France.

I did well in business school, completing the first year of a three-year course with distinctions in all my work. At the same time, I worked as an office junior from 9 to 6 every day – for a paycheck of £64 per week.

What the actual fuck?

I think I was the hardest-working employee in that office. Sorry, Mum. She worked there too and pretty much delegated a lot of chores to me. I didn't mind because it kept me moving. I was constantly running up and down stairs, never sitting still, which kept my anorexic brain happy.

The worst times were when I had to cover reception. Sitting still, unable to leave the phones, threw my routine out the window. I'd literally have a panic attack when I had to do reception.

Even now, I'm not one for sitting still. Writing this book, I have to take breaks every 15 minutes to move around.

One day, we had a temp receptionist who did extra work on TV. She told me I should get into it since I mentioned I'd once wanted to be an actress. But by then, life had happened, and I thought it was just a pipe dream – not something to be taken seriously.

But then my mind started to wander. *Could I still do it? Is it achievable?*

I had just finished my first year of college. Was I about to throw all of that away on a *what if?*

You bet your life I did.

'Manifesting your dreams and taking action leads to endless possibilities.'

One day at work, I picked up a *Yellow Pages* that was underneath the reception desk and started looking for drama schools. I found an ad for The Actors Studio in Manchester, so I picked up the phone to inquire. Andy Devine answered. 'Yes, it's an adult class, Wednesday evenings for three hours.' I was 17, but I was in.

I got the bus into Manchester for my first class, which was more of a preview to see if I liked it. There were about eight adults in the class, and the room was set up like a theatre, with a stage and rows of chairs stacked like you'd see in an actual theatre. I loved the rawness of it.

Andy – who, for anyone reading this, played Shadrach Dingle in *Emmerdale* – was my mentor. Sadly, he's no longer with us, but learning from him is why I am the actress I am today and why I've had longevity in this business. I wish I could have told him what he did for me, but I like to think he knew.

It was 1995. After that first class, I knew this was it. This was what I wanted to do. So, I promptly quit my job and my college course and threw myself into it.

All the money I'd earned as an office junior went into paying for my classes – something I'm extremely proud of. No one helped me. I did this for myself. I believed it would happen for me. I never doubted it.

After starting the classes, my childhood dream of being famous quickly shifted into something different. I didn't want to do this to be famous anymore. That was something the child in me wanted all those years ago. Now, I wanted to learn a craft – because that's what it is. And you never stop learning. Even to this day, I'm still learning.

The course was 90% stage work. Welcome to Method Acting: the Stanislavski system. At the time, I didn't have a clue what that was, but I quickly learned. I was taught to use and believe any emotions or behaviours I had, adapting them to a character under imaginary circumstances. It draws on a high degree of realism.

I learned to pick an emotion, create a character and a scene based on that emotion, and bring it to life on stage. That was our homework, and we performed every week. The course had different stages, including 'The Dark Level' and 'Madness.'

I soaked up every note I was given. The way Andy taught gave me all the tools I needed.

* * *

In the year I was there, I turned 18 – but I looked about 14. I was still 84 lbs and had eating issues, but I was stable. I had a food and exercise routine that I stuck to.

While I was there, I performed in a couple of shows. The second one was a showcase for agents. I performed extracts from various plays and scenes I'd written and performed in class. Afterwards, I was immediately snapped up by the agency Piccadilly Management.

I couldn't believe it.

I had an agent after just a year of quitting college and my job.

This was the beginning of my 28-year career (so far) in the business.

Although I had an agent, I still had to work to earn money, and I still had the rest of my course to finish. I took up some bar and cleaning work at my local pub. I loved it there. I looked so young, though, that nobody believed me when I told them I was 18 while serving their Boddingtons.

On weekends, the pub was really busy – the place to be on a Friday and Saturday. There were lots of us working at the bar, all around the same age. It felt like a little family. I made a lot of friends. I still get the odd DM on Instagram asking if I used to work at The Station Pub, and yes, that was me, back in 1996.

Believe it or not, my first-ever audition was for *Hollyoaks* – for the role of Jude Cunningham. It felt like a bit of a cattle market, full of girls who looked like models. I thought, *I can't compete with them.* So, I just read my lines and left. I knew the role wasn't for me, so I wasn't too upset when I didn't hear back. The part went to Davinia Taylor, who would later become an integral part of my life.

* * *

Unbeknownst to me, while I was busy building the life I'd always dreamt of and things seemed to be settling down, something ugly was about to take over my life in a big way.

I wasn't a party girl. I didn't drink and I didn't smoke – though I'd tried both over the years, as teenagers do. It's a rite of passage. I remember one time, not long after I'd left treatment, when I went out with a group of school friends. We were just hanging around the park, as we did back then.

Some of my friends were drinking, and for some reason, I thought it would be a good idea to join in. I drank a quarter bottle of vodka in about ten minutes, thinking I'd be fine. Spoiler: I was not fine.

I had to be carried home. God knows what my mum must have thought, seeing her not-so-good girl turn up paralytic 30 minutes after leaving the house. Needless to say, I've never been a vodka drinker since, and to this day, the thought of an apple and walnut salad still makes me want to vomit.

* * *

In the midst of all the exciting opportunities surrounding me, my great-grandmother passed away from a stroke.

I was extremely close to her. I spent half my childhood at her house in Chapel-en-le-Frith, Derbyshire. Every school holiday, my sister and I would be packed off to stay with her. I absolutely loved it there. She constantly fed us. The biscuit tin was never empty, and the kitchen always smelled of cakes – especially chocolate chip buns.

All I did there was eat. It was comforting.

It really saddens me that she never got to see me make it as an actress, but I'd like to think she knew I would make it happen for myself.

When I went to see her in the hospital just before she passed, she looked so small in the bed. She never opened her eyes, but I got to say goodbye. Afterwards, I went with my dad and sister to her house to go through her things, looking for anything we wanted to keep that held meaning for us. We filled up some boxes and went home.

That's when it happened for the first time.

As I unpacked one of the boxes, I came across some tins filled with biscuits and cakes. I looked at the biscuits and thought, *One wouldn't hurt.* I ripped open a packet and took a bite of a chocolate digestive. Then I felt an unbelievable urge – something unlike anything I had felt before. I devoured the biscuit. But it didn't stop there. Before I knew it, the entire packet was gone.

Oh my God, what have I just done? I thought, panicking. I had just eaten an entire packet of biscuits – something I'd done regularly as a child without a care in the world. But now? Now this was outside the rules. Now this would make me fat.

I quickly ran to the toilet and, for the first time in my life, tried to make myself sick. I didn't know what I was doing. I just gagged, and some of the biscuits came back up – but not all of them.

What the hell had just happened?

I frantically exercised, overwhelmed with guilt. But something inside me clicked – almost like a jigsaw puzzle falling into place. My messed-up brain thought it would be a wonderful idea to do this again. And again. And again.

In my mind, I could eat whatever I wanted and just throw it back up with no consequences.

Boy, was I wrong.

What started as a packet of biscuits soon turned into raiding entire cupboards, then whole shopping bags – but that came much later. In the beginning, I was sneaky: a few chocolates here, a couple of packets of crisps there. At first, I was terrible at making myself sick – I just couldn't do it properly. But you know what they say: Practice makes perfect.

As I began to audition properly, I became a regular on the circuit, going for some amazing shows. More often than not, I got a recall, but I never quite landed the part. It's almost always down to a look – providing you can deliver a performance, of course.

I handled the rejection quite well – until I auditioned for *The Ward*, a revamp of *Children's Ward*. I had four recalls for a part with Pam Alexander, who was the casting director at Granada TV.

I remember sitting with Pam, and she said to me, 'Oh, you're seeing June on Monday.'

I had no idea what she was talking about.

June West was the casting director for *Coronation Street*, alongside Judy Hayfield. After my meeting, I went to my agent's office, where they told me June wanted to see me for *Coronation Street*.

Oh my God, I was ecstatic. It's every northern actress's dream to grace those famous cobbles.

On Monday, I was prepared. I remember reading for June, and as soon as I finished, she quickly got up from her chair and called Judy into the office. She asked me to read again for Judy.

This was a good sign, I thought.

Why else would she ask me to read again for the other casting director? I knew I'd read well. I left feeling certain it was going to be a yes.

But as I waited and waited, the phone didn't ring. Finally, a week later, they called my agent. Sadly, it wasn't meant to be. They had gone a completely different way with the character.

I was devastated.

I had imagined myself in that role, finally making it. But in hindsight, when I watched the show, the character was an annoying brat who didn't last long. I took that as a sign – that role wasn't meant for me.

Not long after that audition, I landed my first-ever TV role. It was for a Network First documentary for ITV about Peter Sutcliffe, the Yorkshire Ripper. I was cast as his youngest victim, Tracey Browne, in a reenactment of her attack.

Tracey was the only one of his victims to survive. He got spooked by a car after hitting her over the head with a hammer, so he tossed her into a field and fled. Thankfully, Tracey found help.

I met her for research, and I can't thank her enough for being so open with me about what happened.

I remember stepping onto a proper set for the first time. It was a night shoot, filmed close to where the attack actually happened. It was so much fun. I dressed in '60s clothes and spent most of the night covered in fake blood.

I gave it my all, studying and learning as much as I could during those few hours.

When the paycheck arrived, it was a lot – £380. For me, back then, that was a fortune. It was the most money I'd ever earned in one go. Needless to say, I banked it and saved.

I was a good little saver – for a while, anyway.

CHAPTER 4

Hello Cindy

Not long after I finished my first job, I was helping out at my agency's office. It was a co-op, and all the actors chipped in from time to time. I was looking through the breakdowns to see if there was anything suitable for me, and there it was: Cindy Cunningham, 15, youngest daughter of the Cunningham family. I thought, *This is me.*

I asked my agent to put me up for it, and it wasn't long before Dorothy Andrew, the casting director at the time, asked me to audition again.

I got the train from Manchester to Liverpool and made my way to Mersey Television, home of *Brookside* and Phil Redmond's new creation, *Hollyoaks.* The show had been on Channel 4 for a year, starting in October 1995, airing one episode per week. I hadn't really watched it, but I did tune in just to see who got the part of Jude, which I had originally auditioned for.

After its first year on air, *Hollyoaks* was commissioned by Channel 4 to air twice a week.

The character of Cindy was already in the show, but the actress who had played her quit to pursue other projects – luckily for me.

As I entered the familiar room where I had auditioned earlier that year, I noticed there were a lot of girls there. They were all much younger than me, probably around 15. I was 18 and the oldest in the room. My heart sank. *What if I'm too old?* I thought, even though I looked about 14.

The other girls were reading the script out loud while I kept to myself, sitting in a corner and reciting the words in my head. I was the last girl to go in.

Nervously, I sat down as the series producer, Jo Hallows, introduced herself and asked what I'd been up to. I remembered my first audition when I blabbed on about working in a pub. Not making that mistake again, I quickly said, 'I just filmed a documentary for ITV.'

Dorothy read the script with me, and I was being filmed. I fluffed my lines.

Oh no, I thought, as I quickly picked up where I left off and carried on.

When I finished, they smiled and thanked me for coming in. I didn't try too hard or come across as desperate. I just smiled, thanked them for their time, and left.

I hopped on a train back to Manchester and decided to wander around the city centre for the afternoon. After spending most of the day shopping – or window shopping, to be precise – I got the bus home. It was just after 6 p.m. when I opened my front door and saw the answering machine flashing.

Back then, I didn't have a mobile phone. They'd been around for a while, but I'm always late to the party with technology. I get set in my ways, then something changes, and I have to learn it all over again. I'm very old-fashioned like that.

I hit the button.

It was my agent, asking me to ring him as soon as I got the message, which had been left at 1 p.m. The agency shut at 6, and it was now 6:05 p.m. on a Friday. I needed to know what this was about.

I called immediately, and thank God he answered. I'll never forget the words that followed:

'How would you like to be Cindy Cunningham for the foreseeable future?'

'What???' I screamed. 'Is this for real?'

'Yes, Steph. They called as soon as you left the audition.'

I was stunned. That almost never happens. I'd expected at least a week's wait for a callback. But to be told the same day that I had the job? A job I knew would change my life?

At that moment, I felt like I'd achieved everything.

Some would say I manifested this, and I think I did. I didn't know how my life was going to change; I just knew I was excited to be doing what I'd always dreamt of – and to have achieved it, even after doubting whether it was realistic.

I would no longer be that girl who was bullied in school, the loner, the freak.

I proved to everyone – and to myself – that I was somebody.

That I would be seen.

That I would no longer be invisible.

I started filming in October 1996, and my first day was on the Cunningham set. However, the Cunningham set was filmed in a house on Brookside Close. For anyone who doesn't know, *Brookside* was the hit Channel 4 soap set in Liverpool. It was so controversial at the time that everyone was hooked.

I remember turning up for filming and walking across the tiny cul-de-sac, soaking it all in. In my head, I kept saying, *I'm in Brookside Close.*

It really was a pinch-me moment.

My first episode was episode 54. I'm currently filming episode 6396, so as you can imagine, a lot has happened in between.

When I arrived on set, I was taken to makeup – which I loved. It all felt so glamorous, having someone pamper you a little, making you look your best. Trust me, over the years, those makeup artists really put their skills to good use. After makeup, it was a quick trip to costume, where Cindy's school uniform was hanging, waiting for me.

It felt very odd to be playing a schoolgirl, but I embraced every last bit of it. Then I was taken to set by the runner, the third AD, and that's where I met Sarah Jayne Dunn for the first time. She was to be Cindy's best friend, Mandy.

Sarah was a lot younger than me – she was 14, while I was 18 – and at that age, the difference was huge. Not so much now (I mean, I'd kill to be 42 again), but at that time, there was a world's difference in terms of where we each were in our respective lives. She was still at school, had a tutor on set, and was chaperoned by her mum, Dorothy, who I adored. Dorothy was like a second mum to me at that time.

I really liked Sarah. She was mature for her age, very beautiful, lovely, and kind – something she's always carried herself with. *Hollyoaks* was Sarah's first job too, so we were pretty much learning together. That's the great thing about working on soaps – it really is like a school, then a university, before it becomes your career. Eventually, it becomes second nature. You get to the point where you can learn a script in two minutes with your eyes closed.

It wasn't long before I was filming scenes at Mersey TV, where the rest of the sets were. The Dog in the Pond set was so tiny back then – literally half the size of the one they have now. And, of course, there was the main set: Hollyoaks Village. It housed Mr C's Driving School, Drive and Buy, and Tony's video shop, which is where Cindy famously gave birth to Holly on Christmas Day in 1997.

I remember the first time I walked into the Hollyoaks green room. I saw Nick Pickard, Will Mellor, Terri Dwyer, Jeremy Edwards, and Davinia Taylor. I felt so small walking into that room on my own, surrounded by the famous faces I'd seen on TV.

I had never met anyone famous before.

I was so nervous. They all had a shorthand with each other because they'd been in this together for a year. They were a family, and I was like the long-lost second cousin nobody knew about, asking to be let into the fold.

I was shy but eager to please. I wanted so badly to be one of them.

As I said hello to everyone and introduced myself, that's when I saw her: Davinia.

I have never in my life seen anyone more beautiful than her. She smiled at me as I said I was playing her sister, Cindy.

What I didn't expect was her personality – and boy, did she have it in bucketloads. She was warm and down to earth, spoke fast, and had a wicked sense of humour. At that point, I didn't know what we were going to become.

In the beginning, I wasn't immediately included in the group. Even though I was an adult at 18, I think some of the cast saw me as the school kid I was playing – not old enough to hang out with the grown-ups.

But it didn't take long for my naïve little brain to be easily led into a lifestyle that was beyond my comprehension – and really wasn't me.

I didn't know anything about life as a grown-up.

Not until the day Davinia took me under her wing.

In the fast-paced world of soap, once you jump on the train, it doesn't stop until you decide to get off – or you're booted off. Luckily for me, I was on the train, and I was loving every minute of the ride. Or so I thought.

I had a passenger on board with me: the ugly monster, the devil on my shoulder.

As I started making friends with the cast and saw the money rolling in – which was insane for an 18-year-old fresh from the sidelines – things began to shift.

The first year I was on the show, Cindy was more of a recurring character, along with Mandy. We didn't have much to do other than be annoying little sisters to our siblings, who were more central to the storylines. I was still finding my feet, doing my best to put everything I'd learned at The Actors Studio into my character.

The first time I had to cry on screen was in a scene with Lisa Williamson, who played my eldest sister, Dawn. The story was that Cindy had gotten her nose pierced, it got infected, and Dawn gave her a bit of a talking-to. I remember being so nervous about crying. I had to pull something out of myself – something real from my life that made me sad. It was horrible, bringing real emotions to the surface.

Thank God for tear stick!

It's a little trick most actors use to bring on the tears, and it's our job to sell the emotion. I use it, and I don't care what people think. In the fast-paced world of soap, we can't sit around while an actor listens to 'The Wind Beneath My Wings' in the corner, trying to squeeze out a real tear. We need to get it done – and do it over and over again.

Now, don't get me wrong. Over the years, I've used my own emotional state when the story and the writing demand that rawness to really sell the scene. But it's different if you're doing a drama, a film, or theatre, where you have the time to nail the emotion in the right way. In soap? You just get that stuff in your eyes and bawl like a baby. And if you manage to produce snot, that's a bonus – and maybe even a soap award nomination.

After a couple of months, I was called to have a meeting with Jo, our producer. I sat down nervously in front of her. I was actually scared of this woman.

To me, she was powerful, clever, smart, no-nonsense – and she held my career in her hands.

I always felt flustered in her company. I could feel myself trying so hard to please. Cool, I was not. To this day, I think she could still make me sweat a little.

Anyway, as I sat there, trying not to make sweat puddles on her lovely white sofa, she told me I was going to be given a very important storyline – one close to her heart. Cindy was to lose her virginity on her 16th birthday and fall pregnant. Not only that, she was to keep it a secret. The only person she told was the father, Stan (Lee Stanley), who was then killed off in a car accident right after hearing the news.

This was *Hollyoaks'* first big stunt. My character was the catalyst, setting things in motion and leading to the deaths of two of the show's regular characters – Stan and Ollie. For the *Hollyoaks* fans who don't remember, they were *the* original Max and OB.

I was over the moon.

Finally, I had something I could sink my teeth into, and I knew this storyline had legs, meaning I'd be staying another year.

Me and Dee

Think of the movie *Clueless*. Davinia (Dee) was Alicia Silverstone's Cher, and I was Brittany Murphy's Tai. I remember Davinia joking about this once and calling me her 'project', just like in the movie. I didn't take any offence. I was happy to be anything to her.

Davinia saw something in me.

We got on so well, like real sisters, and quickly became inseparable. I instinctively took on her personality – I was like a sponge. But bear in mind, our lifestyles were completely different. Davinia's family was extremely wealthy, so while she shopped on Sloane Street in London, I was shopping at Topshop in the Arndale Centre in Manchester.

Off the set, Davinia showed me what it was like to be a soap star in the '90s – with a bit of cash and a little bit of fame. Back then, there was no internet, no social media, and no camera phones. Getting in the newspapers was what made you.

We had it good back then. We could pretty much do whatever we wanted (within reason) without it becoming public knowledge. Any photos we took had to be developed, so we waited a week to see our memories.

I quickly became accustomed to dinners, drinking, smoking, and shopping in Gucci.

We went to clubs, but we were more dinner-and-drinks girls. The place to be at the time was Mash and Air in Manchester. Anyone who was someone was there – pop stars, soap stars, footballers, models. And I was among them.

We'd eat in Air, the posh bit, ordering Taittinger Rosé and smoking our Camel Lights. Then we'd head downstairs to Mash Bar and party the night away.

It really was the fast lane for me.

I didn't know how to slow down at that point. My whole life had changed so much. I was still living at home with my mum in a two-bed terrace in Flixton, Manchester. I would commute by train to the studios, which was a pain in the ass. It used to take me forever, and I had to be up at the crack of dawn to get there in time for my 7:30 a.m. makeup calls.

I was never late, though. I always turned up on time, knew my lines, and never called in sick. My life had a routine, and I was coping with it – but something was wrong. I had a passenger: the monster on my shoulder.

With earning a lot of money came more freedom – freedom to buy food, a lot of food, bags of food – all of which would end up in the toilet bowl. I had everything I'd ever wanted, but a switch had flipped in my brain. I'd nearly killed myself to be thin, and now I was devouring anything I could get my hands on and making myself sick.

It started slowly because I was living with my mum, and it was hard to do without being caught. This was a secret – a big secret – that no one knew but me.

When I was offered a full-time contract, I decided to move to Liverpool. Having my own flat meant I had free rein to be fully out of control. After a while, it became physically noticeable. I was gaining weight at a rapid pace, but my brain kept telling me, *Just be sick, and you'll stay thin.* It was happening right in front of my eyes, but I couldn't see it. My face became rounder, and my glands were so swollen it looked like I had two golf balls stuck in my throat.

While Cindy was pregnant and hiding her bump, I was growing too.

It would've been believable if I were pregnant in real life – but I wasn't. I gained 42 lbs in one year. I was so unwell, but no one said anything. No one called me up to the office to ask if I was okay. Not one friend, not even my parents. They knew, but because I didn't say anything, neither did they.

Living in Liverpool was great for the commute. Still unable to drive, I would taxi in. I did attempt to take my driving test, but I never studied for the theory, so I failed a few times. I never had time to book driving lessons because I was filming so much – or at least that's what I told myself.

To be honest, I probably did have time. I was just lazy.

I had become so dependent on someone else driving me to work, and this new disease zapped all my energy – along with the partying.

I did love a good party with the cast.

At the time, the cast was so small that the girls lived in one big house, and the boys lived in another on the same cul-de-sac. Either the girls would throw the party, or the boys would. Those were the days – the glory days.

The best times were when I was with Davinia, especially our trips to London. Most of the time, we stayed at the Metropolitan Hotel, which housed the then-famous Met Bar. Anyone who was anyone went to the Met Bar in the '90s, including Kylie Minogue.

The night I met Kylie will forever stay with me for two reasons: I met my idol, and I almost got fired.

Myself, Davinia, and Natalie Casey, who played Carol, had some press appearances to do in London. We had a full itinerary.

The day we arrived, we were doing interviews for Trouble TV, and the following day Davinia and I were booked to do the entire Saturday breakfast show *Diggit*, hosted by Gail Porter.

We were put up in a hotel, and cars were arranged to take us where we needed to be.

However, Davinia didn't want to stay in the hotel that was organised for us. She promptly booked herself into the Metropolitan Hotel and made reservations at Nobu for Friday evening. Not one to miss out, Natalie and I joined Dee and some of her London friends for dinner.

Nobu is where they filmed that famous scene in *Notting Hill* with Julia Roberts and Hugh Grant – where Julia's character overhears a bunch of sleazy men gossiping about her, gets up, and humiliates them with the line, *'I'm sure you all have dicks the size of peanuts. Enjoy your dinner. The tuna's really good.'*

It was so posh – a great place to play 'spot the celeb'. My first sighting was of Ben Affleck and Gwyneth Paltrow.

The food, however, was predominantly tiny portions of pretentious sushi. I hadn't tried raw fish before, and it really wasn't for me. I scoured the menu for anything chicken and cooked. (Although now, sushi is one of my favourites.)

After dinner, we headed down to the Met Bar, where we drank, and I scanned the room, still deep into my game of spot the celeb. That's when it happened. Davinia came up to me and said, 'You're not going to believe who's here. Kylie!'

My stomach fell out of my ass hearing those words.

'Kylie? Oh my God, where?' I frantically spun my head around the room.

Dee replied, 'She's in the toilets,' and that was it. There was no stopping me. My heart was literally beating out of my chest. As I opened the door to the ladies', there she was – sat in front of a mirror, perched on a cushioned seat, in a beautiful red dress perfectly sculpted to her petite frame. One leg crossed over the other, her hair swept up elegantly. She was holding a compact mirror, reapplying her red lipstick.

I had to be brave. I had to – for once in my life – be *that* girl. The girl who just went for it.

So I did.

'Excuse me,' I said, and then, all sense of coolness left my soul as I blurted out, 'I love you!'

I gushed about how much of a fan I was and mentioned that I was an actress on TV – just so she wouldn't think I was a total loser and could maybe, somewhat, be relatable to her. Maybe I could be her best friend? No, Steph. Back down to earth.

All I remember was her thanking me, standing up, and giving me a big hug.

For me, that was enough. It was a moment I'll never forget.

Kylie would have been so used to strangers coming up to her, asking for autographs, wanting a piece of her. While she'll never remember that moment or who I am, I want her to know she made all my inner child's nine-year-old dreams come true.

Back at the bar, I floated on Cloud Nine, reciting every last detail to Davinia. I don't think she was that bothered. Dee knew plenty of famous people and was very much into R&B and house music, while I was fully pop.

That night, I ended up staying with Davinia in her hotel room. God knows what time we went to bed, but we were supposed to be up and ready for 6 a.m. for the car that was driving us to Buena Vista Studios for our Saturday morning stint on *Diggit*. 'Supposed to' being the operative word.

Did I hear an alarm? No. Did Dee hear an alarm? No. Did the random stranger asleep on the tiny sofa hear an alarm? No.

Our phones were ringing non-stop. It was our head of publicity, Diane.

When we finally woke up and saw the many missed calls and voicemails, one word summed up the situation: ***FUCKKKKKK.***

It must've been around 7 a.m. We scrambled, grabbing our things, makeup still on from the night before, clothes too – it was like doing the walk of shame on national TV. Davinia got us a taxi, and all I remember was legging it as fast as we could down the street to the studios, trying to make it before the show ended.

When we arrived, we were greeted by Fearne Cotton and a very young Holly Willoughby before being rushed through makeup. We were definitely still drunk.

We ended up doing the last half hour of the show. Somehow, we pulled it off. Together, we were funny – you couldn't help but laugh at our enthusiasm and energy. Dee was quick-witted, while I played up to saying stupid things that came across as sweet and endearing. It was a role I'd forged for myself. The more airheaded I appeared, the more people laughed – not at my expense, though. It worked.

But that wasn't the real me at all. I *am* and always have been very intelligent.

After the show, we got the train back to Liverpool. During the journey, we knew all hell was about to break loose at work. Diane, the head of publicity, was effing and blinding on the phone, saying Jo wanted to see us in her office first thing Monday morning – and that our jobs were on the line.

Davinia told me not to worry, that she'd take the blame.

I spent the rest of the weekend drowning in anxiety and fear.

What the hell had I just done? Had I thrown away my career because of my partying?

Well, I *did* just meet Kylie.

That wasn't the point.

My life was already spiralling out of control. I just couldn't lose my job on top of that.

Monday morning came, and Davinia and I took a seat outside Jo's office. Through the window, we could see a TV positioned high up in the corner of the room. She was watching *Diggit*. Both of us were so nervous, but as we watched her, we could see her laughing.

Maybe this won't be as bad as we think? I hoped.

Davinia was the first to go in. This wasn't the first time Dee had been reprimanded – more often than not, it was for lateness, which is a big no-no in this industry.

As I sat there, I tried hard to listen, but I couldn't quite hear what was being said. After a few minutes, she came out, and true to her word, she told me she'd taken the blame – that none of it was my fault.

I breathed a sigh of relief for what my friend had done for me.

I wasn't out of the woods, though. Jo still kicked my ass a bit, and I was given a warning – a warning I should have listened to, because that wasn't the only time I got into trouble for doing live TV pissed.

CHAPTER 5

Feeding the Monster

My job was safe, and I was into my second year of *Hollyoaks*. I had given birth to *Hollyoaks'* first-ever baby, Holly, and I quickly became a central part of the cast with my own storylines rather than just being a vehicle for someone else's.

This was also the year that marked the beginning of the era of the *Hollyoaks* girl and boy – an influx of sexy twenty-somethings cast as students to fill the new university and halls of residence, as well as a big new family, the Patricks. I didn't like change. I was still trying to fit in with the current cast, and now I had to compete with the likes of Joanna Taylor and Dannielle Brent. They were all stunning.

I, however, still had my head balls-deep into a toilet bowl.

At this time, my bulimia was at its worst. I was being sick almost every day, and if I had a day off, I'd spend it bingeing and purging. I still didn't get that I was piling on the pounds, not losing them. I'd drink so much water after a binge to help bring up all the food, but my body was still soaking up thousands of calories.

A *Hollyoaks* girl, I was not.

This is one of my biggest regrets – how much time I wasted during that period of my life. But honestly, I'm not sure I had a choice. Mental illness isn't something you can just say no to. Even though I *knew* I was putting on weight, I was powerless to stop the endless binge-purge-guilt cycle. The dopamine hit I'd get from every binge was like a drug. I was an addict.

I still believed I was managing to hide it, but people obviously knew.

I remember one time I was staying with my dad at his pub. I had a binge day, and he banged on the door of my room, then barged in as I quickly tried to hide the evidence. I failed. He literally dragged me out of the room, put me in his car, and drove me to his motorhome by the lake not far from the pub. I hadn't had the chance to be sick. I ended up sneaking out for a walk, hoping I could bring it all up without being caught. But I couldn't do it. I had to let it digest.

My mind was so consumed, all the time, with thoughts of food and when I could plan my next binge.

I had trigger foods. If I ate a sandwich at tea break on set, then I'd feel like I *had* to bring it up – but not before eating ten sandwiches, ten chocolate bars, ten bags of crisps – you get the gist. If I ate any food I deemed 'bad', that was the trigger.

I'd feel awful after being sick, and the next day, I'd be dehydrated and weak.

It's really hard to look back at old episodes of myself looking that way. During the first lockdown in 2020, *Hollyoaks* started showing fan-favourite repeats because we'd run out of new episodes. Back in the '90s, there was no social media, no chat forums, and no *Daily Mail* comments section for people to tear you apart.

I felt sick knowing those old episodes were about to surface. I knew how I looked would be an all-you-can-eat buffet for the keyboard warriors dying to tear me apart for not fitting their idea of perfection.

I begged *Hollyoaks* not to put the clips on Instagram. They did – but they deleted any nasty comments so I wouldn't see them.

As 1997 came to a close, *Hollyoaks* was fast gaining its now-famous reputation as the sexiest show on TV. We had that market covered – well, the other girls did. The lads' mags came knocking. Lads' mags built careers. Getting a photoshoot in one of those meant you'd made it, and we all wanted to be in them. I, however, wasn't asked in the beginning, and because of my weight gain, I was happy to sit on the sidelines and watch Davinia, Joanna, and the others take the lead.

Although every part of me wanted to look like them, *be* like them.

Once again, I was back in the playground – the odd one out. My weight meant I wasn't pretty enough, good enough, or skinny enough. Being slim meant beauty, adoration, and attention. Sex appeal. So, naturally, I believed – yet again – that to be loved, I had to be thin.

That wasn't happening for me anytime soon, not with the devil still calling the shots in my head.

However, in 1998, *Maxim* magazine planned a photoshoot with *all* the *Hollyoaks* girls, including me. We were going to be on the front cover and in a pull-out feature, with each of us having our own page inside the mag, along with a small interview. This was my first, and I was ecstatic. Finally, I was noticed. Finally, I was a *Hollyoaks* girl.

I remember the shoot so well. Looking back now, I realise I wasn't overweight. I was bigger than I'd been when I was anorexic and slightly bigger than the other girls, but I was not fat. I have to remind myself of that when I look at the pictures. I wore a tasteful set of underwear and did some great shots. They even took Polaroids so I could see them, and I looked beautiful. I was so pleased with how they turned out. Everyone was happy.

But then, before the magazine came out, I got a call from our publicity department. They apologised and said they couldn't use my photos in the front cover pull-out because my underwear was a different colour from the other girls'. They also told me I'd be sharing a page with Dannielle – who'd also get her own page. I would not.

I was devastated.

I didn't understand. My underwear was the same colour as everyone else's, and even if it wasn't, they could have digitally changed it. It confirmed what I already believed: the fat girl from *Hollyoaks* isn't good enough to be on the front cover of anything.

This hit my confidence hard. All these beliefs I'd placed on myself were being confirmed by others.

When the magazine finally came out, I absolutely loved my picture, and I'm very proud of it. It taught me a valuable lesson – your truth is your own. If you believe you're beautiful, no matter what anyone else thinks, you can begin to unwire the limiting beliefs that you're not.

Stop wearing other people's opinions like clothes. We put them on, layer by layer, until they become a second skin. We feel so heavy under all that weight of judgement. Take the damn clothes off.

Years later, I finally did. I graced the front cover of a top lads' mag – on my own.

Time to Say Goodbye

It wasn't my goodbye, though. It was Davinia's.

I'm not sure what happened – it isn't my story to tell – but Dee was leaving the show. I was heartbroken. Losing my friend, my one true ally, felt like losing a part of myself. She'd taught me so much and shown me a world I'd never known. Even though I realised that world – the fast lane – wasn't really for me, I'd tried so hard to compete, to fit into a lifestyle that wasn't mine.

By then, I'd burned through all my savings. I was overdrawn, with no money to pay my tax bills. Everything was gone on designer clothes, shoes, expensive gifts for my family, trips to Marbella, luxurious hotels in London.

I don't regret any of it. I lived my young adult life. But I *do* wish I'd lived it for me. I wish I'd known who I was and owned it. I wish I didn't have the monster in my head.

Okay, so there are a few regrets. But meeting Davinia? That's not one of them.

It would be a good 15 years before we saw each other again.

Dee moved to London and became fast friends with Kate Moss and the London elite – so far out of my league that it was inevitable we'd drift apart.

Part of me was relieved. I finally had space to look at myself, to try and figure out who I was.

But before that, I had one last lesson to learn.

My dad had rebuilt his pub into a nightclub in Winsford, Cheshire. He was having an opening night and asked me to come along and bring some of my celeb friends to help drum up publicity – which I did. A few of my friends from *Hollyoaks* and *Brookside* came along. I don't remember much about the night, but what I *do* remember is that *The Big Breakfast* was coming to Mersey TV the next morning.

Oh, it'll be fine, I must've thought, as I hadn't been to bed all night and decided to get a taxi from Winsford to Liverpool in the early hours. Lord knows how I managed it – these days, I can barely manage two drinks before needing to go to bed, only to wake up the next day feeling like I've been run over.

When I arrived at work, *The Big Breakfast* crew was setting up in The Dog in the Pond. I went straight to makeup to refresh myself and then tried to act like a normal human being for the next two hours while we were interviewed live on TV. I don't remember anything out of the ordinary happening. I pretty much kept my head down and let the others do most of the talking. When I was asked a question, I don't recall slurring my words or being asked to repeat myself.

When the show wrapped, I breathed a huge sigh of relief – I'd gotten away with it. I got a taxi back to my flat and face-planted straight into bed.

No sooner had I closed my eyes than my phone rang.

'Steph, it's Lisa (Jo's PA). Jo wants to see you in her office now.'

'Right now?' I replied, still half-asleep.

'Yes, now.'

I hung up and immediately called a taxi. Adrenaline shot through me as I tried to convince myself this could be good news – maybe my next big storyline? But anxiety quickly filled me, replaying the last time I was in Jo's office and got a warning.

Fuck, fuck, fuck.

When I arrived, I peered through her office window. She was at her desk with a TV positioned high up in the corner of the room, playing *The Big Breakfast*. Gently, I knocked on the door.

'Come in!' she called.

I opened the door and sat down on her now very familiar sofa.

'Hi, Jo. How are you? Everything okay?' I asked nervously.

'No, everything is not okay,' she snapped. 'Stephanie, you were pissed.'

Fuck. Full-named. This was bad.

How did she know? I thought I'd hidden it so well.

Desperately, I tried to defend myself, explaining I'd been at my dad's opening night and hadn't slept because I was nervous about the show. But Jo wasn't buying it.

I was in trouble.

I have to thank Jo for this, though, because that woman saw something in me – potential I hadn't even seen in myself at that point. She could see I'd been swept up in the fast lane with Davinia, but she also saw that, at my core, I was a bloody good actress who always delivered on set.

So, Jo gave me my last and final warning: shape up or ship out. Oh, and I was banned from doing any publicity for the foreseeable future.

Fair play.

So, I shaped up.

I decided I needed help for my bulimia. I found an eating disorder centre in Liverpool and started outpatient treatment. Once again, I was back in therapy, rehashing all the events of my life to try and pinpoint the needle in the haystack that would explain why I was mentally ill.

Would talking about these things somehow magically take away the intense craving to binge? Would I suddenly have a lightbulb moment where I'd realise I *am* worthy, I *am* loved, and my self-worth is not tied to my thighs? Would that instantly give me a normal life?

I didn't even know what normal looked like.

It wasn't until three years ago that I began to create a life with boundaries and conditions – a life where I made agreements with myself that I couldn't break unless I allowed myself space to be free.

I managed to tame my addiction, at least somewhat, as I continued with the show. I started working out and restricting food between binges – which, of course, was to my detriment, because restriction always leads to bingeing.

Regardless, I kept my head down and cracked on with my job. Over the next couple of years, I got some great storylines and kept my partying to a reasonable minimum – just weekends with my group of friends in Manchester who weren't on the show.

I still had a good time, but I never drank on a school night again.

It was the beginning of 2000, and I'd done four years on *Hollyoaks*. I'd been offered another year-long contract, but something inside me wanted more. I kept thinking, *Do I stay another year?* Something was pulling me to say no. There was so much more I wanted to experience in this business – other characters I wanted to bring to life. I wanted to push myself out of the comfort zone I'd grown so used to and just see what would happen.

So, I bit the bullet.

I went to see Jo and told her, 'Thank you for the offer of another year, but I'd like to leave at the end of my current contract to pursue other things.' I made sure she knew how immensely grateful I was for the opportunity she'd given me, even when I'd messed up.

Jo was so lovely to me, wishing me all the best, and so commenced my exit storyline.

Cindy's departure saw her three-year-old daughter, Holly, mistakenly ingesting an ecstasy tablet while Cindy had brought her to work at The Loft because she couldn't find a sitter. Social services threatened to take Holly away, so Cindy, with the help of her boyfriend Ben (played by Marcus Patrick), fled to Spain on a private plane.

And that was it. Cindy left *Hollyoaks* in November 2000.

CHAPTER 6

Crashing in a Palace, Down Under

When I left *Hollyoaks* after four years, the only way I can describe it is I felt free. There was no doubt in my mind that I'd made the right choice, and dare I say it – I was happy. I was back to what I believed was my purpose: developing my skills as an actress, playing different roles, and embracing the wonder of where it all might lead me. There I was, out in the world, the unknown ahead. I had no fear.

I'd moved to a new agency that was based in both London and Manchester, so I had the best of both worlds. Most importantly, I believed in myself, just like I did when I was at The Actors Studio or auditioning for the role of Cindy. I knew I'd work again, and I hadn't been in *Hollyoaks* so long that I'd be typecast – it was the perfect timing for me. It was meant to be.

I was in a routine, living with my boyfriend Ben, who I'd been with for a year. I'd lost a lot of the weight I'd put on when my bulimia was at its peak. I'd bleached my hair blonde and, for the first time in my adult life, I actually felt hot – even sexy. I still had bulimia, but it was in remission and only surfaced occasionally.

After a couple of months of auditioning, I got my first job back on TV. It was an ITV drama called *A&E*. It was just a guest appearance for one episode, but it was enough to get my feet wet and back in the game. All my scenes were with the lovely Jane Danson, best known for her role as Leanne Battersby in *Coronation Street*. I'd known Jane over the years since we'd both been in soaps, and it was a nice little job that made me thirsty for more.

Not long after filming *A&E*, I got a call about a new drama being cast starring Ricky Tomlinson called *Nice Guy Eddie*. They wanted to see me for the part of the protagonist's youngest daughter, Laura. I was sent the script in the post to read through.

On the day of the audition, which was in Liverpool, I felt back on familiar turf. I had to do a Liverpudlian accent and read a couple of scenes handpicked from the script. I didn't even know I *could* do a Liverpool accent until it just came out of me – subtle, not the strong Scouse you'd hear on *Brookside*. I thought it went well, and they must have too, because I got a callback.

The second reading was in front of the executive producers and writers. I dressed casually in low-rise jeans and a blue cropped T-shirt. I spotted a couple of well-known actresses at the audition, which made me doubt myself. My inner monologue was relentless: *What if they like her better? She's probably more suited for the role than me.*

I'm always a bag of nerves for auditions, but this time especially so, because I wanted the role so badly. You can't help imagining what it would be like to get the job and how it could potentially change your life. Still, I did my thing. There wasn't loads to read, but I did what I felt was a solid job. Not long after, my agent called. I'd got the part.

Once again, that feeling swept over me – the same feeling I had when I booked *Hollyoaks*. I was so excited. This was a series for BBC One, and it felt like my career was heading in a new direction. The first episode was just the pilot to test audience reception before the green light for a full series, so the wait for news was long.

Walking onto the set of *Nice Guy Eddie* was daunting and very different from my time on *Hollyoaks*. Like I said, *Hollyoaks* was like a school, and it taught me so much technically, so at least I knew what I was doing. Meeting Ricky was incredible – he was larger than life and full of stories. I was a bit starstruck, having grown up watching him as Bobby Grant in *Brookside* and later in the hit show *The Royle Family*.

Playing my long-lost brother was Tom Ellis, who has since gone on to smash Hollywood as the lead in *Lucifer*. It was a strong cast. Filming scenes took much longer than on a soap. The lighting setups were more intricate, and we didn't shoot as many minutes per day, so we had more time to get each scene just right.

After the pilot wrapped, my next big job was already waiting in the wings. To me, it was my dream job. If I'd ever had even a flicker of regret about leaving the security of *Hollyoaks*, I'd remind myself: *You wouldn't have done this if you'd stayed.*

Next stop: Down Under – Sydney, Australia. My boyfriend at the time, Ben, was an actor too, and we had the same agent. An audition came in for him for the part of a British bad boy in a Sky One show called *Crash Palace*, about backpackers in Sydney. The thought of him getting the job and leaving me for four months filled me with anxiety. So, I asked my agent, on the off chance, if there were any parts for girls being cast. It turned out they were looking for an 18-year-old party girl from Essex named Tina. I had never tried an Essex accent before, but I thought I'd just blag it and told my agent I could do it. I just wanted to get in the room and be seen.

On the day of the auditions, Ben and I headed to London to Sky, where they were being held. I dressed the part: a very short denim skirt, a pair of red heels, and a red tank top with rips held together by safety pins. My hair was cut short, very bleach blonde, and styled in a messy, swept-forward way, a bit like early Meg Ryan. As I signed in at reception, I couldn't help but notice the list of names – and there it was: Dannielle Brent.

Dannielle was in *Hollyoaks* with me, and she was from Essex, a dancer, blonde, and absolutely beautiful. My heart sank. *Well, that's it*, I thought. *The part is hers.* But I wasn't about to fall at the first hurdle when it came to auditioning. I just had to push past my nerves, stop overthinking, and go for it.

I remember it so clearly – sitting in that room with a bunch of people asking me questions, a camera pointed at me. I kept thinking, *Relax, you can do this.* Then I started with the accent. *Fuck,* I thought. *This is not going well.* So, I stopped and asked if I could read it in my own accent first, then try the Essex accent again after. To my surprise, they agreed. Halfway through my read, I thought, *Do something out of the box. Something no one else would do.* So, I pulled a small comb out of my pocket and started teasing the back of my hair as I provocatively played out Tina's lines.

After that, they said there was no need for me to do the accent – what I'd done was fine. At the time, I wasn't sure if that was a good or a bad thing. And with that, I left. The tapes were sent off to Australia for the producers to review. It became a waiting game, and as the weeks went on with no word, I convinced myself I hadn't got the part. When you don't hear back, it's almost always a no.

Then, out of the blue, the call came. My agent, Claire, said, 'You fancy going to Australia for four months? You got it.'

'What?!' I screamed down the phone. 'For real?'

Claire replied, 'Yes, for real.'

Oh my God, I couldn't believe it. I was 23, had just shot a pilot for a BBC series, and now I'd been offered an amazing role filming at Fox Studios in Sydney – with a four-year option, meaning I could potentially be travelling back and forth to Australia for the next four years. My life, once again, was changing, taking me on a trajectory I hadn't expected.

Looking back, this was before we all knew about *The Secret* and asking the universe for what we want in life, but I was doing it. Everything I had ever asked for, I got – including anorexia. Hence the saying, *Be careful what you wish for.* It's mind-blowing.

I do believe some things in life are destined to happen to us, even the bad, to get us where we need to be. I firmly believe that if I hadn't been through half the shit I have, I wouldn't be where I am, or who I am today. Who knows – maybe I could've been a better version of myself and still lived out my dreams without the mental health struggles and eating disorders. But honestly? I wouldn't gamble.

It was May 2001, and I was off to Oz. Sadly, Ben didn't get the part of the bad boy. I was told I'd be meeting the actor who did at the airport, and all I knew was that his name was Warren. When I arrived with my two huge suitcases, I looked around for where we were supposed to meet, and then I heard a very familiar voice booming towards me. As I turned to see who it was, I couldn't believe my eyes – it was Warren Derosa, who had played the baddie Rob Hawthorn in *Hollyoaks*.

'OH MY GOD!' I shouted. I loved Warren! We'd never worked much together – our characters were worlds apart, and our storylines never overlapped – but I'd always thought he was incredibly talented. Posh, too. He was very well-spoken, and he looked just as surprised to see me, especially since I was about 42 lbs lighter than the last time he'd seen me. I was 23 and in the best shape of my life. My eating habits were still quite restrictive, but I wasn't anorexic again. I was stable. The monster only reared its head occasionally, but before going to Australia, I'd been fine for a while. Maybe I'd kicked this?

We boarded the Malaysian Airlines plane and were seated in business class – something I'd never experienced before in my life. The meals were full white-table service, with an array of Malaysian dishes to try. My seat went back almost horizontally, and it was so wide you could have fit two of me in it. That was also the first time I ever wore an eye mask and earplugs – two things I still can't sleep without to this day.

Catching up with Warren and sharing the excitement about what was to come was fun, but I decided the best thing for me was to sleep as much as possible. I've never been a great sleeper. It was about 13 hours to Kuala Lumpur, where we'd change planes for the rest of the 24-hour journey to Sydney. I remember stepping off the plane feeling like I was on a boat as we walked through the airport. We had a four-hour layover, but Warren found us some internet access – not that I knew what to do with it, as in 2001, the internet was still pretty alien to me. Like I've said before, I'm always late to the party when it comes to technology. He also found some fancy massage chairs for business class passengers. Bliss!

When we finally arrived in Sydney, I stepped out of the airport, took in the air, and instantly felt like I was home. I've always thought I belonged in Australia, like I must have lived there in a previous life. When I was two years old, my parents had visas to move us out there, but something changed last minute, and the move was cancelled. I don't know what happened, but I could've been on *Neighbours* and actually become best friends with Kylie! One can dream.

Warren and I were picked up by a driver and taken to what would be our home for the next four months: Medina on Crown, a hotel/apartment complex in Surry Hills, right in the heart of Sydney. When we checked in, we excitedly made our way to our rooms. As I opened my apartment door, my mouth literally dropped to the floor.

There was a double bedroom to my right with a huge bathroom next to it. Straight ahead was the living room with two sofas, a coffee table, and a TV. To the left, the kitchen adjoined the living room and was fully stocked with everything I'd need. There was even a guest bedroom on the other side of the apartment with another bathroom. It was huge. My room was at the front of the building and had patio doors that opened onto a small balcony overlooking the city.

Warren's room was just across the hallway – like something out of *Friends*. However, on closer inspection, Warren's apartment was much bigger than mine, with a massive balcony that could've been a second living room. I was a bit jealous, but I made mine feel like home, and I loved it – except for the city noise at night. That's where my trusty earplugs came in handy.

The first night we were there, we were told we'd be having dinner with Jimmy Thomson, the man who created *Crash Palace*, the man who cast us. We were so jet-lagged, but it didn't matter – I was excited to get out there and feel like a grown-up in Sydney. The dinner was lovely, and it was great to get to know Jimmy. He was Scottish, very warm and engaging, and I was eager to impress him. Of course, the first thing I did after my drink arrived was light up a cigarette, not realising Australia had already implemented its smoking ban. Oops. That was embarrassing when I was told to put it out. I thought they were joking! England hadn't caught up yet.

Jimmy talked us through the show. It was about backpackers staying at the famous Sydney hostel, *The Royale*. Almost every character was a different nationality, though the cast was predominantly Aussie. It was a very adult show, airing late at night past the watershed, which meant swearing and nudity were fair game. It was gritty and real. Jimmy then casually mentioned that I looked a lot different from my tape. Panic started bubbling up. He said I was curvier than he imagined and a lot smaller in real life. I'd lost a bit more weight since the audition, but I didn't think it would be a problem. Luckily, it wasn't. Phew. Jimmy also told me he hadn't even reviewed anyone else's audition. I was the first one on the tape, and as soon as he saw me, he said, 'That's our Tina.'

Later that evening, when Warren and I got back to our apartments, I got a call on the landline. A Scottish voice boomed down the line – it was Jimmy. I had no idea why he'd be calling. He began by saying it was so lovely to meet me, but seeing me in person wasn't what he'd expected from my tape. My stomach dropped. He said he was really sorry, but I'd have to get on the next flight back to London. I couldn't believe what I was hearing. I started crying, struggling to catch my breath, when I suddenly heard a laugh – a very familiar laugh. It was Warren playing a practical joke.

I hung up the phone and flew into his apartment, punching him in the arm. 'You fucking dickhead! You had me!' My heart was still racing as he roared with laughter. That was the beginning of our sibling-like relationship, something I'll always treasure.

After a night's sleep and battling dreadful jet lag, we were up early to head to the studios for our first read-through and to meet the rest of the cast. When I say 'studios', I mean the 20th Century Fox Studios, where actual movies are made. Our set was right next to where *Mission: Impossible* had been filmed, and *The Matrix* was on the same lot.

When we arrived via taxi, we were given access lanyards and shown to the set. We entered a room filled with tables arranged in a big square for the table read of the first few episodes. That's when I saw him. *'Oh my God,'* my inner 14-year-old whispered. It was Dieter Brummer, the guy who played Shane in *Home and Away* in the early '90s – back when I used to rush home from school to watch. I even had a poster of him on my wall. Of course, I kept that to myself, at least until I got drunk and decided it was a great idea to let him know I'd had a huge crush on him.

I introduced myself and quickly found a seat within his eyeline. It wasn't long before the room filled with people – the cast, writers, and producers. Toby Truslove, who's Australian but was playing my British best friend Brian, sat next to me. I loved Toby from the get-go. He had such a quick wit and made me laugh so much. We clicked straight away.

I loved every single one of the cast members. Most of them were Australian and had been on TV for years, so I recognised a few faces. We were all around the same age, and I immediately felt like I fit in – something I'd never felt during my time on *Hollyoaks*. There, I always felt like the underdog or like I wasn't liked. Looking back, I think it was more that I didn't like myself and projected that onto others.

But here, no one knew me. It was a clean slate. There was something so relaxed and easygoing about this cast. There didn't seem to be any egos or cliques. Everyone had time for each other. We quickly became like a family, spending as much time together off set as we did on.

After the table read, it was so fascinating to hear everyone in their characters, most of whom were playing different nationalities. I was so impressed. One girl, Tory, whom I became the closest to, was just stunning – and I mean stunning. Long blonde hair, model looks, sun-kissed skin – her face was flawless, not a single open pore. Meanwhile, I had so many skin issues. I'd started getting acne, probably caused by my eating disorder, so I was forever covering up the bombs being dropped on my face. I didn't dare go without foundation or concealer. I wished every day for perfect skin, just another thing that made me feel unattractive. Tory was playing an Argentinian character called Inez, and her accent was as sexy and flawless as her skin. There was so much talent in one room. I was itching to get started.

After a break, Warren and I went for a walk outside. There was a grassy verge ahead of us, which we were told would be the spot for our Friday barbecues. Just past it, we spotted Michael Caine. He was filming *The Quiet American*. Neither of us dared to say hello; we just stood and watched. He looked so in the zone. It's such a nice memory to have, though the story would've been a much better anecdote if it had gone something like, 'I met Michael Caine on my first day on the job, and he gave me a cameo in his new film.' But no, all we did was watch him until we were called back in.

I settled in quickly and found myself with a new bunch of Aussie mates. Dieter was lovely, but I didn't fancy him – which was strange, considering my teenage crush. It's mad, isn't it, how personality and who you click with are often more important than looks? And obviously, I had a boyfriend back home, but it's always nice to window shop.

All the interiors for the hostel were filmed at Fox Studios. I'd often walk to the studio listening to my compact CD player. The weather was always nice, even though it was wintertime. It wasn't hot enough to tan, but it was still pleasant. We shot anything outdoors at various locations around Sydney. The first one I remember was a beach scene at Coogee Beach. It was stunning – but cold. Too cold for me, anyway. I'm always cold. If I don't have a hot water bottle strapped to me, people ask if I'm okay. It's always horrible filming scenes where you have to pretend it's hot while wearing next to nothing, trying to hide your goosebumps. But you just suck it up and act your ass off.

I loved location filming. Getting to experience parts of Sydney while being paid to do so was a dream. Over the coming months, I got to know my way around. I'd often go to Darling Harbour for lunch. Shopping in the city felt like being in London, but with the added beauty of beaches dotted around. It was the best of both worlds – and so cheap. Well, it was in 2001. It was three dollars to the pound back then. I couldn't believe it. I loved getting my money's worth, especially with clothes. I've only recently thrown away some of the things I bought there. I'm such a hoarder, but holding onto those clothes felt like holding onto the memories of being there.

So, let's talk about Tina. Tina was fun – a party girl with no responsibilities. She was 18, just looking to meet boys and party her way around Sydney. She arrived with a bang. I loved playing her. She had such a free spirit, and her style was very edgy. We were even allowed to smoke in scenes, which added realism to her character. The drinks, of course, were alcohol-free. There's just something about TV sets and smoking back in the day. Everyone smoked. If you didn't, you'd almost get a side-eye look. Every cup of tea was accompanied by, 'Ooh, let's have a fag.' Smoking in scenes was great – it made me feel like Carrie Bradshaw, lighting up in almost every scene of *Sex and the City*.

With Tina being a pocket rocket of a wild child, it was inevitable that I'd have to film my first sex scene. Nervous is an understatement. The actor I was playing alongside was quite famous in Australia, had been in loads of roles, and was considered a heartthrob. I, however, didn't fancy him – he really wasn't my type at all. It's a shame because it always helps with chemistry in romantic or sex scenes if there's even a tiny spark, as long as you know each other's boundaries.

It was a closed set, so very few people were there. It was also the first time I'd ever been naked on camera. All I had on was a G-string. We were lying on Tina's bed, which was the bottom bunk in the girls' dorm of the hostel. As he lay on top of me, I could feel his nerves. I just remember thinking, *Just go for it, be professional, do what's scripted.* The scene called for Tina to have a really loud orgasm – so loud it could be heard throughout the hostel. Talk about being thrown into the fire! Not only did we have to simulate sex, but I also had to fake an orgasm. Luckily, that bit I had nailed (pun intended). And then it was over, thank God. I'd done it. All I could think was, *I really hope my parents don't watch this.*

Tina's story got very intense. My next sex scene was a whole different ball game. I was given a rape storyline where someone climbed on top of Tina while she slept, starting to have sex with her after she'd been put to bed drunk. She tries to push him off, but she's too drunk and weak. After that, Tina flees the hostel.

With Tina missing, I had some time off from filming. I didn't do anything crazy. There was no partying like in my *Hollyoaks* days. Sure, we went out for a few dinners and hit a couple of clubs, but that was about it. I remember one particular dinner – it was a cast member's birthday, so we all went to the revolving restaurant in the sky, Infinity at Sydney Tower. That was a fun game. Every time we wanted a cigarette, we had to go down 81 floors just to light up. By the time we came back up, our dinner table would be on the other side of the restaurant.

I didn't have a huge break before I was back on set. However, having some downtime and being on my own allowed the bad thoughts to creep back in. The cravings kicked in. *Just one biscuit,* I told myself. But no, it was never just one. It started again. I promised myself I wouldn't do it – that I wouldn't let this disease control me and ruin my time here – but I was powerless to stop it. When it comes back, I don't feel like my usual bubbly self. I become introverted and feel unable to be me. I want to hide away from other people's normality because it only reminds me of how far I am from normal.

Not long before leaving Sydney, I got a call from my agent. 'Good news,' she said. '*Nice Guy Eddie* has been given the go-ahead for series one – six episodes starting shooting in November.' I was on Cloud Nine. I'd been hoping it would be picked up, and now it had. I could see my future mapped out so perfectly: shoot *Crash Palace*, then *Nice Guy Eddie*. Two regular roles, splitting my time between the UK and Sydney. What more could I ask for?

But even with everything I'd ever wanted, I was still making myself sick. Was I not happy? What was it that I so desperately needed in my life to end this self-inflicted misery? It boiled down to one thing: the ability to accept that food wasn't my enemy. Sadly, that acceptance was still a long way off.

September rolled around quickly, and it was time to leave. I didn't want to go. Being in Australia had been the best time of my life. But I knew it wouldn't be long before I'd be back for season two. I'd acquired so much stuff while I was there that I ended up leaving a suitcase with Tory to hold onto until I returned.

What I didn't know then was that it would be the last time I'd ever see my Australian family again. After the show premiered on Sky One and Foxtel, it wasn't renewed for another season. Everything I thought was going to happen – everything I'd planned for – wasn't to be. But at least I still had *Nice Guy Eddie* – right?

CHAPTER 7

The Spotlight and the Shadows

Back home, and it was promotion time. I had a shoot with *FHM Australia,* the first shoot I'd done since the awful experience with *Maxim* magazine. This time, it was just me, Tory, and Kristy Wright, who played Chloe in *Home and Away* back in the '90s. The girls did their shoot in Australia, while I did mine in London. I'd lost a bit more weight – I don't know how, as I was still bingeing and making myself sick. Maybe I was 'doing it right' this time? Remember what I said about practice makes perfect? Who knows. But I was tiny again, around 84 lbs, like when I first started *Hollyoaks.*

I loved the shoot. It was elegant and sexy, more editorial than glossy. I was airbrushed to death, of course, but I absolutely loved the pictures. Afterwards, it was a stay overnight in London, followed by a screening of the first couple of episodes of *Crash Palace,* press interviews, and then dinner with Warren. It was so lovely to catch up with him, even though we hadn't been home long. Only he knew what we'd experienced over there, so being with him felt comforting.

Unfortunately, Warren left to go to America, and we eventually lost touch. We communicate sometimes, but it's rare.

I continued doing press for *Crash Palace*, hitting all the shows – *Lorraine*, *The Big Breakfast* (where I was actually interviewed on that famous bed), *T4*, the popular Sunday morning show that was perfect hangover TV, to name a few. It was exhilarating being the face of the show in Britain, as Warren was in America. There was no social media back then, so promoting a show meant getting on TV sofas and into magazines. That's why the lads' mags were so useful to us back in the day – they were how we promoted ourselves and our work.

My next shoot was for *Loaded* magazine, featuring 'Girls of 2002.' The spread showcased women to watch that year, and I was one of them. I had the centre spread, wearing red underwear and lying across a bed. When the issue came out, I hated it. I don't know why. But I still have the magazine, and I'm proud of it now – I look hot.

Crash Palace aired on 10/10/01 at 10 p.m. on Sky One and ran for a few months. I'm not sure what the audience numbers were, but when I learned we weren't being renewed, it felt like all I had left of my time there were those episodes. That show and the experience will always hold a special place in my heart and will forever remind me why leaving *Hollyoaks* was the right choice.

Recently, I found a diary from when I returned to England after *Crash*. Piecing the timeline together from all those years ago has been bittersweet. What I thought would be a nostalgic look back has made me feel sad for my 23-year-old self.

Extract: 1 September 2001

'Today is being ill day, just gonna be ill, do nothing, and try to recover.'

'Tomorrow will be a life-changing day. I know I say this all the time, but I need to start putting my life into perspective, stop putting things off.'

'Today has been the worst day. I hope things are better tomorrow. I know I always say things are going to change, but they never do. Maybe it's time I start looking after myself and those I love.'

'Didn't get the *Casualty* job. Apparently, I was their first choice, but the producer decided to go with someone with a West Country accent. It's okay – it just means I have the time to promote *Crash Palace.*'

2 October 2001
Food Eaten Today:
Breakfast: 1 pear, 1 low-fat yogurt.
Lunch: Tuna salad.
Dinner: Prawn stir-fry.
Supper: 1 pear, 1 low-fat yogurt.

The food diary I kept reads pretty much the same every day, with slight variations of low-calorie, low-fat meals. No wonder I was so thin – I was taking in way under 1,000 calories a day and exercising like a maniac. Bulimia was my body's way of screaming for more calories, craving food to survive. Why, oh why, did it take me another decade to listen?

4 October 2001
'The only thing I have to do today is go for a medical for *Nice Guy Eddie* in Manchester.'

'Claire called and told me that Catherine Willis (*Casualty*) said I was great, blah, blah, blah, and that they'd like to have me as a regular character starting in November. But unfortunately, I'm busy. Nice, though.'

15 October 2001

Doctors Appointment: 3:20 p.m.

'Okay, great thinking, Steph. I'm so stupid for thinking this could be the last time I'd have a bad day before going to the doctor, hoping she'd sort everything out. Well, I was wrong. She was a complete bitch to me, with no sympathy whatsoever. In fact, she made me feel worse – like I had no self-esteem left. Why do doctors do that to you? They're supposed to be nice.'

'Maybe she's right, though. Maybe I can only save myself if I really want to – and I do, so badly. But I still need to speak to someone more than anything. I need to ask, *How can you help me?*'

'Why will talking make me better?'

'Isn't there some miracle?'

'Something has to be done. Nearly ten years have gone by, and I'm still no better. Instead of defeating myself, I'm going to try – starting tomorrow. Every time I get an urge, I need a distraction. Maybe I'll leave the house and go for a run or have a bath, put on music.'

26 September to 15 October: *7

I would always put a star at the top of a diary page as a symbol for a bad day, meaning I had binged and been sick. Seven times in just over two weeks.

23 October 2001

'Cast and crew meal in Liverpool for *Nice Guy Eddie*.'

'Today didn't exist for me. I am a victim of myself. I battled with myself, and the bad side won. I deserve to feel the way I'm feeling right now. I don't deserve to go out with everyone. It was my choice; no one forced me.'

'I hope tomorrow will be a good day.'

24 October 2001

'Episode 5 of *Crash Palace*.'

'I really should go swimming today, get out of the house and do some exercise.'

'Today wasn't good. I already knew I was going to have a bad day because I planned it in my sleep. Why? I don't know. *Loaded* came out today, and I hated it. That gave me an excuse to have a bad day so I could ignore it.'

'I've come to a decision – one I seem to make every day of my life. No more. From now on, I'll change my diet, introducing new foods and not eating so much in one sitting, to reduce the size of my stomach because my stomach capacity is too large.'

'I'm going to write down everything I eat at the end of the day. I'm also going to exercise every day in different forms, trying not to let myself get stuck in a routine. Drinking water every day.'

'Today may have been bad, but it may also have been an awakening – hopefully. *Nice Guy Eddie* starts soon, and I need to be fit for that. I'll also weigh myself once a week. I didn't lose the two pounds I put on last week – why didn't I lose the weight? Maybe I eat too much.'

After this date, my daily extracts stopped for a while, which is what I always did over the years of keeping diaries. I'm all in, and then I leave it. It's like that with most things: I'm hyper-focused, and then something happens, and I just stop. Then I regret the things I didn't do – like the television drama I wrote about being in the Unit. I have touted it around, received interest, but haven't followed it through. Maybe this is a sign that I should add *'screenwriter'* to my bio.

Filming commenced for *Nice Guy Eddie*. We filmed six episodes over four months. I was pretty much living in the Holiday Inn Liverpool during filming. I spent most of the shoot in a school uniform. I remember being on set one day when a security guy asked me where my chaperone was. He couldn't believe it when I told him I was 24 and main cast.

Filming was done during the winter, from November 2001 to February 2002. It was freezing. There was no green room or studio; we were mostly on location, with a base comprised of trailers. We each had our own, with our names on the doors.

I spent a lot of time in my trailer reading *Harry Potter*. I was never much of a reader, but I got through the entirety of the first four novels during filming. Yes, there was that much waiting around. It was far from glamorous.

We had a few familiar northern faces as guest stars. Joanne Froggatt, best known for *Downton Abbey,* played my best friend for an episode. Even David Walliams made an appearance.

2002 was a great year for my career – I was flying. Auditions were coming in thick and fast, and I was seen for some incredible shows. Even the ones that didn't go my way, I came so close to getting them. I auditioned for the recast role of Tracy Barlow in *Coronation Street.* I was recalled for the role and even had a screen test in the Rovers with Jimmi Harkishin, who plays Dev. I nailed it. I was almost certain I'd got the part. Even the casting director gave my agent positive feedback. But I looked like a teenager at 24, so it didn't go my way. I wasn't surprised the role went to Kate Ford, but it proved the right decision. She was the perfect Tracy.

Instead, I went on to film guest roles in *Mersey Beat, Holby City,* and *Doctors.*

Sadly, *Nice Guy Eddie* didn't get renewed for a second series, just like *Crash Palace.* I often think back to what my life could've been like if those decisions – made by one person – had gone the other way. I don't like to dwell on it. Would I be happier? More successful? Would I have never gone back to *Hollyoaks?* Would I have gone to America? Who knows – the *what ifs* are endless. All I know is that the journey is forever changing, and sometimes embracing the bad takes you to the place you need to be to find the good.

2003 was a quieter year, although I was asked to play my first role without having to audition in a new ITV drama, *Sweet Medicine,* starring Jason Merrells and a few other famous names.

Toward the end of 2003, although it had been a quiet year, I was given my own class to teach at The Actors Studio. That income was enough to keep my head above water. I was still in and out of remission, but I was managing to keep my addiction under control. Then something else happened – something unexpected, out of the blue, and impossible to hide. It kept me isolated from the world.

It was September, and I was in the hairdresser's when I got a call from my agent asking if I'd be interested in going back to *Hollyoaks.* It was for 12 episodes. The story was that Cindy's dad, Mr C, and her stepmum, Helen, had died in a car accident, leaving behind a will, and she was coming back to claim what was rightfully hers. I accepted the offer, and filming was to begin in January 2004.

As the end of the year approached, I started to get a bit of acne. This wasn't unusual. As I've said, since having an eating disorder, my skin has always been bad. I was never without spots. I had even begun to accept it. It was an everyday cover-up job. Someone at a beauty salon recommended the skincare range Dermalogica to me, saying I needed to use their anti-bac face wash along with some of their other products if I wanted to get rid of my acne. So, I bought everything she suggested. I would've tried anything.

Not long after I started using it, boils began to appear on my face and neck. Every day, more and more showed up. They were sore – from the tops of my cheeks, across my jawline, and down my neck – red raw pustules. I was disgusting. I was desperate. There was nothing I could do – they just kept growing.

Anyone who's had acne will understand what I was going through. I didn't dare touch my face – not even the whiteheads I used to get pleasure from popping. I was too scared of scarring and creating potholes in my skin. I officially had the worst bout of adult acne. I was an absolute mess.

I didn't dare binge or make myself sick either – for fear I'd make it worse. It felt like everything I'd done to myself had shown up on my face for the world to see. I cried every day. I'd lie on my bed, trying to watch TV. I remember watching the *Sex and the City* box sets on a loop. And every five minutes, I'd get up to look in the mirror, examining myself to see if the acne was going. It only made me cry more.

My mum kept telling me that stress and crying would only make it worse. That really didn't help. I thought this was me forever: disgusting, ugly, and disfigured.

I went to the doctor, and they prescribed me antibiotics. I didn't have long before I was due back on the *Hollyoaks* set – four years after being away. I wanted to blow their minds with how I looked and how successful I'd been since leaving. Not in a braggy 'look at me' way, but I wanted them to see I wasn't the fat loser I thought I was. But with these mountains on my face, the last thing I wanted was to be on camera. I didn't want to see anybody. I'd become a recluse. Makeup couldn't cover it; there was no hiding the lumps.

The time had come. Scripts had arrived, and I got the call:

'Hi Steph, your call time for tomorrow is 7:30 a.m. Makeup. Costume at 8:10 a.m. On set at 8:30 a.m. Scene numbers 1199.05 and 04.'

I remember this like it was yesterday. As I arrived in the makeup room, I felt small. My hair was long and blonde, and I wore it in a centre parting so the sides could cover my cheeks. As I sat in the chair, Nick

Pickard walked into the room. For anyone who hasn't watched *Hollyoaks,* Nick plays Tony – the original character – and still does.

'Hello, darling, how are you?'

I took one look at him and burst into tears, saying, 'Don't look at me.'

God knows what he must've thought. To this day, I've never brought it up with him, so he probably doesn't even remember. All I did was cry. I didn't want to be there.

The makeup girls were brilliant. They used Estée Lauder Double Wear and a heavy concealer palette to cover everything up. The DOP (director of photography), who's responsible for lighting, made sure I was always in the shade – which is unheard of, because we're always told to find our light, and if we're shadowed, we have to redo the take. They really looked after me.

But I just couldn't wait to get home at the end of each day's filming. It was terrible when it should've been the best time ever. I was coming back to a show that taught me so much and was responsible for my growth into the adult world. All those dreams I'd had of being accepted as a *Hollyoaks* girl? I couldn't give a flying fuck about them. I just wanted to be as invisible as possible, do the 12 episodes, and fuck off. Which is exactly what I did.

After filming wrapped, I went to see a private dermatologist who said I qualified for Roaccutane, a strong treatment for severe acne. Finally, something worked. It took a few months for the lumps to clear and for the redness to calm down. Luckily, I didn't scar in a way that was noticeable. I could only tell when I was in the sun – my face would tan except for the white marks left behind by the lumps.

Over the years, I've had laser treatment to help with the scarring, but nothing's completely worked. Since being on that treatment, though, I haven't had acne again. I still get the occasional spot, but my skin has behaved ever since. Part of me thinks that because I'd always asked the universe for perfect skin, I had to go through the most traumatic bout of acne to get the stuff that would finally fix it for good. That's how I find the positive in that event in my life.

For my next job in 2004, I was cast in a guest role for *The Royal*, a spin-off from *Heartbeat*. It was a great part. I played a pregnant heroin addict named Georgie, trying to get clean for her baby. It was so good to sink my teeth into something so different from anything I'd done before. I worked alongside Natalie Anderson, who had a regular role as a nurse. It was a short stint, but I loved it.

In 2005, I did *Doctors* again, playing a surrogate for a gay couple, but this time, I was pregnant with my first child in real life.

Then, in 2006, I was cast in *Holby City* again, with some fascinating repercussions. The way the universe works to make way for the things you ask for – when you believe they're meant for you – is amazing. While I was filming, an audition came in for *Coronation Street*. The role was for the Christmas double-episode special, with a few more episodes scheduled for March 2007. However, on the day of the audition, I was filming *Holby*. I had one scene at the beginning of the day and the last scene of the day. Instead of being defeated and passing on the opportunity, I went to see the producer and explained the situation. Amazingly, she had the schedule changed so I could film both of my scenes together in the morning and then catch the train straight to Manchester.

It was a tight squeeze: the sheer panic of not making it, relying on public transport to be on time, and the fact that I had no makeup on because that morning I'd been filming an operating room scene, so I looked like absolute death.

Luckily, everything went my way. I made it to Granada TV in the heart of Manchester. As I waited among the other girls, who all had their faces full of makeup, my doubt crept in again. *Shit*, I thought. *Once again,*

I'm not going to be pretty enough to get the job. Once again, I was tying my self-worth to my looks. I even had the sticker marks still visible on my chest from the hospital set monitors.

But guess what? I nailed the script and was offered the job. Finally, I got to walk on that famous cobbled street.

I started with *Coronation Street* in 2007. It was my dream job, and I loved every minute of it. I desperately wanted to be working regularly again. I was growing up, and with that came responsibilities. I had a one-year-old daughter, and I was single. As great as it was doing guest appearances in different shows, the money wasn't reliable. If I got one job a year, it would be a couple of grand at most.

There's a huge misconception about how much actors get paid. Yes, a soap opera role with regular episodes pays well, but it's per episode. So, if you're not in a major storyline and just pop up occasionally, it's not mega money. Some weeks, you might earn as little as £200, while others you could make up to £5,000. It balances out. If you land a series, that can be well-paid too, but it depends on your status and how bankable you are with the audience.

It makes me so mad when I see articles about actors taking a 'normal' job, as if that's some kind of failure. It's utter bullshit. Bills need to be paid. When I was pregnant, I took a job with the NHS to support myself. Would that have been deemed a failed career if it had been public knowledge? No.

As short-lived as my time on *Coronation Street* was, the universe said YES to me again. Just a couple of months after filming, I happened to be at the 2007 Soap Awards. That year, *Hollyoaks* pretty much swept the board for the first time ever. I hadn't watched the show in years, so I didn't know most of the cast, apart from a few who were still there from my time.

As I was walking out of the auditorium to the after-party, I bumped into Bryan Kirkwood, the executive producer of *Hollyoaks* – the man who put the show on the map and the reason behind their awards victory.

He said, 'You're Cindy?'

'Yes,' I replied, astonished that he even knew who I was.

He then said, 'We've just been talking about bringing Cindy back. Would you be interested?'

Now, I had never thought about going back to *Hollyoaks* again. I really thought it was in my rearview mirror, especially after my prior experiences with the show. But, to my surprise, my gut told me to go for it.

'Yes, I'm interested,' I said.

Bryan replied, 'I'll be in touch.'

And that was it – for a year. I heard nothing. I'd pretty much let it go and didn't think it was going to happen.

Until March 2008, just under a year later, my agent got the call. I was offered the chance to play Cindy again. I accepted.

Sixteen years later, I'm now preparing to say goodbye to Cindy once again.

Between 1996 and 2008, I experienced both the security of full-time, long-term employment as an actress and the unpredictability of jobbing year in and year out. As much as having a full-time job was great for the security and the chance to do what I loved every day, the goalposts shifted. When I left *Hollyoaks* in 2000, it was because I wanted something more for myself. I could have stayed for the paycheck, but that's all I would have been doing it for – and at that time, it wasn't about that for me.

When I left *Hollyoaks*, I was in debt. For me, it was about finding what made me happy. And although I battled my inner demons along the way, I don't think I ever really found my happy, even when I landed the jobs I went for. Sure, it was an exhilarating dopamine hit of acceptance –

of being good enough, of being chosen. It validated that I had the talent. But the feeling was always fleeting.

Fame never brought me any kind of happiness either. That elusive thing you think, as a child, will bring you adoration and fortune – it's not real. I've never had that level of fame, and I don't want it. Whenever I'm in the press, being talked about, it just fills me with anxiety. Sometimes you have to play the game, but it's such a double-edged sword.

There are countless things outside of myself that I thought would bring me happiness, but the one at the top of that list has always been love.

PART THREE

What's Love Got to Do with It?

CHAPTER 8

Chasing Butterflies

As the title of the famous hit song by Tina Turner asks, what's love got to do with it? For me at the time, the answer was: EVERYTHING! Love, to me, was the Holy Grail of happiness, and I have been in full pursuit of it my whole life. The first time I ever felt that bolt of lightning in my stomach, I was 11 years old.

I will never forget it. It was the first day of high school, and the first time I had ridden the bus. As I stepped on and paid for my ticket, I looked around for Lucy, who I was meeting. It was then that I saw him – a blonde boy with the loveliest face I had ever seen. All of a sudden, my stomach flipped, and I felt sick. I spotted Lucy and quickly sat down. I didn't say anything because I had no idea what I had just felt, but I knew I fancied him.

It wasn't long before I found out his name: Antony. Antony and his friend Stuart got the same bus as Lucy and me. We went to Flixton Girls School, and they went to the boys' high school, Welacre. Every day, we'd see them. Lucy fancied Stuart, and he fancied her. I never thought in a million years Antony would fancy me. I was *the fat one*, remember?

I used to daydream in class about what it would be like to be his girlfriend. I would graffiti my books with *Steph 4 Antony*. I had no idea what these feelings were. The rush of hormones every time I saw him – I thought that was love. *Is this what it feels like?* I would wonder.

Looking back now, your desire to want something so much, and then the thought of not having it or losing it, creates a fear in you that feels like butterflies – or maybe it's anxiety. There's a fine line between the two. The butterflies come from attraction, and the mind quickly creates a fantasy relationship. When it doesn't happen the way we imagine, it turns into anxiety and rejection. We learn this at an early age, and it's a cycle we repeat well into adulthood.

It wasn't long before all four of us were hanging out at the park near my dad's place, where I lived above my grandma's record shop. Lucy and Stuart quickly became a thing.

Then, one day, out of the blue, Antony asked me out. I couldn't believe it. Was it a joke? Maybe it was. I'd had meaner jokes played on me before. But it wasn't – he was serious.

This was, without a doubt, the best thing that had ever happened to me. The boy I had dreamt about finally asked me to go out with him, which back then just meant holding hands and snogging in bushes.

When I said yes, it was inevitable – I was going to have my very first kiss. I panicked. We were in the park, and I said to Lucy, 'I don't know what to do.'

She said, 'Just open your mouth and touch tongues a bit.'

Touch tongues? I thought. *Ewwww!* Nope, I'm not doing that.

Then it was time. He took my hand, and we went into the bushes. We kissed, open-mouthed but no tongue. *Phew,* I thought. I also thought, *Damn, I'm a good kisser.* Together, we just fit.

For the next couple of weeks, it was the same routine: hang out for a bit, then we all went into the bushes. He asked me if he could put his hand under my top – he wanted to touch my boobs. I said no, and he replied, 'I will anyway.' (Not sure how that would go down today.) I let him, and it wasn't as bad as I thought. I was young, and I didn't have a clue what we were doing; I just remember it felt nice to be fancied. Looking back, though, I was just a girl who fancied him. Boys at 11 years old are not that deep: they just want to touch boobs. Girls, on the other hand, are already planning the wedding.

Antony and I went out for about three months in the first year of high school. It ended because he fancied Lucy more than me. He broke my heart, and I fell back into her shadow, once again, as *the not-pretty one.*

Lucy loved it. Who wouldn't want all the boys fancying them? She was still with Stuart, though they were on and off for a while.

In the second year of high school, Antony asked me out again. Let's get straight to the point: another couple of months of the same thing, and – boom – right on time, he dumped me again because he was still in love with Lucy. You'd think I'd have learned my lesson at this point, right? *He's just not that into you.* Where were my *Sex and the City* girls when I needed them at 13? But nope. In the third year (Year 9, as it's called now), I agreed to go out with him again. Do I really need to say what happened?

After the third dumping, I was done. I couldn't take the rejection anymore.

So, let's unpack this. From the age of 11, for three years in a row, I learned it was okay for a boy to give me affection and then take it away, leaving me rejected. Wow. That sounds painfully familiar. It's a pattern I've repeated my whole life. Those same feelings of butterflies from the attention, followed by the rush of anxiety with the rejection, and then tying my self-worth to someone else's validation. It's all bullshit.

If only I'd written this book 20 years ago, I could have saved myself so much heartache and pain. I wouldn't have spent so much time thinking I was the problem or holding onto unrealistic expectations. I don't blame Antony for having feelings for my best friend. What I do blame him for is stringing me along when he didn't really want me. But he was a child. He didn't know any better.

I've never been married, and the reason is because I always believed there would be *the one* – that person who was meant just for me. I thought I'd been in love before, and I'd like to believe it's true – that when I said those words, I meant them. But honestly? I'm not sure I believe that anymore.

How do you even know you're in love? Is it the rush of butterflies? The endless conversations? The incredible sex? The way they treat you? Is it good communication? Acceptance of who you truly are through their eyes? Is it someone who stands by you through the bad times and holds you up when you're down? Is it loyalty?

I think it can be all of these things. Because now, I finally have them all. It's only taken me four decades to find it.

For so long, I thought love was a butterfly, and chasing it felt like a full-time job. But then, as soon as that last butterfly faded, something about the relationship never felt quite right. Arguments started creeping in, along with that over-familiarity where his likes become yours, and vice versa. You start asking for permission to go out with your friends. And somehow, it's your fault if another guy hits on you.

The little things begin to irritate you until they grow into big things. You stop seeing each other's point of view, and one of you always has to be right. I'll admit it: I'm guilty of fleeing when relationships hit the stage of more arguments and less sex.

I've had four long-term relationships in my life. I don't count anything under a year as long-term. Yes, I've had more boyfriends, but for one reason or another, they didn't last beyond a few weeks or months. Either it was my decision or theirs. I thought I was falling fast in a short space of time, but now I know it was just the butterflies and my romanticised imagination of what could be.

I loved dating, though. I loved getting dressed up and being taken somewhere nice for dinner. It was always dinner for me – never just drinks. I liked to get to know the person over a proper meal, especially if we'd been chatting for a while on social media or WhatsApp. I hate that kind of chatting, by the way. I'm very much a people person. I can't gauge what someone's like through technology. If the chat's good, I'll accept the date. If not, I usually just let it fizzle out.

I've been engaged twice but never married. The first proposal was when I was 23 – my first proper boyfriend since high school. My first grown-up relationship. The second? Well, we'll get to him a bit later.

What I'm about to share is purely my point of view on these relationships and isn't meant to belittle what we had together. There are always two sides to every story – my version and his version – and I'll say that about all of my relationships. When you're deep in it, you expect your partner to be on the same page, to know what you're thinking, to be like you, and to meet the expectations you've fantasised about your entire life. But no two people are the same. Each of us has a very different view of the world. How I see an event is rarely the same as how someone else sees that same event.

I didn't know this back then. I had this clear picture in my mind of what love should look like – thanks to movies, love songs, and Disney. Yes, *fuck you*, Disney.

I'm not going to go through all of my relationships spilling secrets for titillation. That's not what this book is about. It's about learning who I was, what I was looking for, and ultimately chasing that butterfly. The one I thought I could catch and keep. The one that fits like Cinderella's shoe. And again, – *fuck you*, Disney.

I met Ben at the Press Club in Manchester in 1999. I was still filming *Hollyoaks*, and Ben had just wrapped on series two of *Queer as Folk*. I recognised him from the first series. I knew most of the cast since they'd been filming in Manchester, and we all hung out together – dinners, parties, nights out in the Gay Village. But I'd never met Ben before.

So, when he came over to me one night at the Press Club, it was an easy introduction. The club stayed open until 5 a.m., so I'm guessing we met around 1 a.m. I remember feeling a bit dejected that night. I always went out hoping to meet someone – a trait I never shook when I was single. One of my friends, Rhian, even nicknamed me 'Meerkat,' because as soon as I walked into a bar, I'd start scanning the room for a man.

Anyway, I wasn't having much luck that night until Ben, full of confidence, bounded over to me. He wasn't my usual type at all. I liked pretty boys – the David Beckham, clean-cut look. Ben was good-looking but in a different way. He was wearing a black beanie and grungy clothes, into alternative and rock music, with a liking for piercings, which I wasn't into at all.

But he was cool – very chatty and confident. There was something about him that drew me in. Maybe it was the fact that he was in the same industry as me. Whatever it was, we hit it off, and we started dating.

Ben was fun to be around, the life of the party. He had a camp side to him that made me wonder sometimes if he fancied men. He'd really play it up whenever we were with our gay friends. He loved being the centre of attention, always cracking jokes and going for the laughs. At first, it was endearing, but over time, it started to grate on me.

I couldn't help but feel like he was trying a bit too hard to make everyone laugh. Maybe it was an insecurity thing on his part; I don't know. This is just my perspective, and I could be completely wrong. It's just how I saw things at the time.

Our relationship moved fast. We became friends quickly as well as lovers, and we moved in together barely a month after we started dating. It wasn't long before we settled into a routine. Ben introduced me to box sets – besides *Friends*, my first real addiction was *Buffy the Vampire Slayer*, followed by the spin-off *Angel*. We'd eat dinner, snack, and smoke while watching episode after episode.

We were together almost a year before I started to get itchy feet. That feeling I'd had in the beginning wasn't there anymore. The excitement of getting to know someone new, the butterflies – it was all gone, and cracks started to form. We argued more, and the compatibility we thought we had at first began to fade. For me, anyway.

By then, I'd left *Hollyoaks*, and the auditions for *Crash Palace* came around. Ben didn't get the part, but on the day I found out my fate, something happened. That particular day, I felt it was time to tell Ben how I really felt. I sat him down and said, 'Ben, I don't think we should live together anymore', basically hinting that I wanted to end the relationship but didn't quite know how to go about it. I really didn't want to break his heart.

As soon as I told him, my phone rang. It was my agent telling me I'd got the part in *Crash Palace* and would be heading to Sydney for four months. Now, any normal person in this situation would've taken that opportunity to move on, be single, and see what was out there – no strings attached. Not me. I panicked. 'I didn't mean it,' I said as I told him the news.

For me, this was amazing news, but I didn't want to dampen it with a breakup, so I reversed my decision. Looking back now, that was a mistake. I should've let him go. He didn't want to break up, and I clung to the comfort of something familiar.

After I'd been in Oz for a month, Ben flew out to see me. While I was at work one day, he was at my apartment, planning something. When I got home, the place was lit up with what must have been a hundred candles. I was in shock. What the hell was going on? He walked over to me where I stood by the door – almost ready to flee the scene (I'm joking, but not really). He took my hand and led me to the sofa. Then, he got down on one knee and proposed.

I was 23. He was 21. God knows what he was thinking. My thoughts were: *You have no bloody money. I'm paying the bills, the rent, your flight, and now you've taken out a loan to buy me the Millennium Diamond?!* Should I have been grateful? No. He was an idiot for doing that. But, honestly, I was an even bigger idiot for saying yes.

At the time, I got swept up in the romance of it all. I wasn't thinking about any of the aforementioned stuff at that moment – though it was there, lurking. How the hell do you turn down a proposal when you're on the other side of the world? I couldn't deal with a breakup, so I kept my mouth shut and went along with it.

When I got home in September, it wasn't long before we split. I just couldn't fake it anymore. I didn't feel the way I thought I should feel. He wasn't my person. We broke up, I gave him the ring back, and we stayed friends for a while. All I can say is thank God I didn't marry him – he's fully gay now and proud of it, too. Like I said, I had a gut feeling.

Looking back, I think age played a big role in my reluctance to settle down. The way my career was going, I was here, there, and everywhere. There was so much to experience, and when it came to love, it had to be right. Surely, true love existed?

In 2003, I was teaching at The Actors Studio. I had a couple of new starters, and one of them was Daniel. As soon as I saw him, I thought, *Oh no, not another model.* He was 21, very good-looking, and just my type. He was four years younger than me, but that didn't stop me from getting to know this young lad who'd turned up at my class. It turned out he was a police officer and the youngest to join the Greater Manchester Police (GMP) at just 18 years old.

I was instantly attracted and impressed. I think it was because he was so normal, and to me, he had an important job – not just a job, a career.

Why on earth was he in my acting class? It was something he'd always wanted to do, and fair play to him, he stuck with it.

As the weeks went on, we got to know each other, and I knew he fancied me. He was, as I remember, a bit shy in that department – something I liked and hadn't experienced before. I'd always gone for the knobhead show-offs who pretty much just use you and then bin you.

After Ben, I didn't think I was looking for anything serious because, well, I wasn't. But I was always chasing butterflies, and with Daniel, I had them by the bucketload. It wasn't long before we started dating, and things between us got serious. I ended up moving into his house – a new-build, two-bedroom place, with a mortgage at 21. I thought, *This is what I need – a man with a bit of security, someone who's not going to sponge off me.* Not that I had anything to be sponged at that time anyway.

I thought I was in love with him. We got on well, but there was something missing. I don't really remember us being friends – we didn't laugh a lot. We slipped into that familiar routine you do when you have a partner. I don't think we were compatible at all; we just went with the flow for a while.

It wasn't until I fell pregnant with my first child, Mia, that things between us started to fade away. He was so young and wasn't ready to be a father, while I was in no doubt that it was what I wanted. Eventually, our relationship started to feel more like two estranged friends, and neither of us can really remember much of those three years together.

Our breakup was the most amicable in the history of breakups. I remember it as clear as day. We were sitting on the sofa, and we both mutually agreed it was time to call it a day – even though we had a one-year-old daughter. Neither of us cried; we just went our separate ways and co-parented our daughter.

What I will say is this: he is the best father to Mia, and I'd like to think the reason we met was so we could be her parents. Maybe he'd think differently. I'm not sure what this relationship taught me. I didn't find my *happy* in the end. In your twenties, you're finding your own feet in life – never mind trying to find the shoe that fits when it comes to a man.

We didn't fit, and that's okay. I don't have any demons from this that made it impossible for me to love or be loved. I simply moved on – to my first-ever boyfriend, Antony.

In 2007, a few months after Daniel and I had split, I had just joined Facebook. It took me a while to cross over from Myspace, but I eventually gave in. Long-lost friends from school, Sydney, and my *Hollyoaks* days were constantly being added. And who should pop up in my friend requests? Antony.

We ended up messaging each other. It was so weird after all those years. I think the last time I saw him was when I was 18 and working at The Station pub. We sent a few messages back and forth until he eventually asked if I wanted to have dinner. I accepted.

I wasn't expecting anything, and I really wasn't expecting to fancy him. We had dinner at EST EST EST in the Trafford Centre. He lived around the corner while I was living in a flat near Farnworth with my daughter Mia, who was two at the time.

All I remember was having a really good night – helped by a lot of rosé wine. The conversation flowed, and we ended up back at his place. One thing led to another, and we slept together. Now, *that* I was not expecting. It felt so natural, so I just went with it.

After that night, we started spending more and more time together. I loved that he had a steady job and his own house. To me, he was a grown-up, while I still felt like a teenager chasing my dreams, never really settled anywhere. I felt comfortable with him and wanted to be around him as much as I could. I really did think I fell in love with him.

We were together for six months. There was no label on our relationship. He never called me his girlfriend or made any kind of commitment to me. He never promised me a thing. I just went with the flow, careful not to put any pressure on him.

But then, one day, I felt uneasy and had an uncomfortable knot in my stomach. Out of nowhere, he said it was over. He told me he felt like he was falling for me but didn't want to be in a relationship, so he had to end it before we got in too deep.

I mean, what the actual fuck?

He had done it to me again. I was sure that this time, my perfect figure and success as an actress would make me a catch he would not be able to allow to slip away. But he did. I was heartbroken, once again at his hands.

Not long after, I was back at *Hollyoaks*. I only ever saw him one more time after that. He begged me to see him again, but I think I'd finally learned my lesson with that one. It was a flat *NO*.

This boy was my first love – the first to give me those butterflies. And I've been chasing them ever since. That feeling is so intense you think it's love. It isn't. It's a chemical shitstorm that can break even the most closed-off humans on the planet. There's no escape from the butterflies, and I love the sensation of every single one.

I've dated many men throughout my life, and if there were no butterflies in the room, there was no second date.

I was single for a year before my next long-term relationship, but not by choice. At that point in my life, I was 30, a single mum, and back in *Hollyoaks*. I thought meeting someone would be easy.

I was wrong.

I just never clicked with anyone, and the ones I fancied didn't fancy me back. I remember feeling so lonely on my own. Most of the cast I hung out with had partners, and I was jealous. I wanted that *new-in-love* feeling again. The butterflies.

Sometimes, I'd catch them, but it would never go anywhere. More often than not, they were created in my imagination – the possibilities of what *might* happen with that person.

On New Year's Eve of 2008, I didn't have any set plans for the night, and I very nearly stayed in. Then the girls in the cast rallied, and before we knew it, we were all meeting up and heading to a club to bring in the new year. I saw Dan walking through the club, and he made a beeline straight for me.

I'd met him a couple of months earlier, and I really wasn't interested when he tried to chat me up then. At the time, he'd been to a christening and was wearing an awful beige suit. He'd been drinking all day, so he was in full overconfidence mode. I just thought, *No.*

However, when I saw him on New Year's, he looked completely different – just jeans and a white T-shirt. Instantly, I found him attractive. As he smiled and said hello, his whole demeanour was inviting. That night, I was interested in getting to know him better. We sat talking for what seemed like hours. It was easy, and I felt comfortable.

Then the countdown came. I remember feeling very nervous. *Shit, he's going to kiss me.* And there it was. In those 10 seconds, a rush of butterflies flooded the pit of my stomach. He kissed me, and it was a good kiss. It was even captured on camera.

It's very true what Cher says in the song 'It's in His Kiss.' If the kiss is bad, then for me, it's not going to work. I almost think a kiss is far more intimate than sex. Everything is in that kiss, especially in the early days when all you do is snog each other's faces off. This is how much pressure I put on myself – and the other person – to be nothing short of perfect and to meet my ideal expectations of what love is.

Needless to say, Dan and I had our first proper date two days later, on 2 January 2009.

When you first start dating someone, more often than not, you fall into the relationship trap. If you agree to a third or fourth date, by then, you're somewhat committed. You may have either slept with each other or are waiting for it to feel special. However, this isn't true of all relationships. Sometimes, you can spend a week with someone and then never see them again. Or one of you just wants to sleep with the other, and then, just like that, they're gone, and you're left ghosted. I've been in all of these situations.

With Dan, though, one date led to another and another, and after a couple of months, he moved into my house.

At this point in my life, being back in full-time work with *Hollyoaks*, I decided to be sensible and put my money into property. I wasn't about to fuck my money up the wall like I did the first time around. Being in a position where you have nothing is scary enough, never mind having nothing with a child to support.

So, for however long this job would last, I was determined to save, save, save. That meant no designer clobber. I didn't buy the bags, the shoes, or the jewellery – none of it. I became the ultimate high-street girl. Fancy dinners and nights out were few and far between. I still loved a night out, but it wasn't every weekend like it had been back in the day.

I was definitely following a pattern with moving in with someone so soon. This was the third time I had lived with someone within a couple of months of being with them. We just wanted to spend all our time together, which is all you want in those early days. But there has never been a truer saying than 'What goes up must come down.'

At the beginning of a relationship, you bring your best self to the table. It's all about impressing and agreeing. You share war stories of past relationships and life experiences, your communication feels like no other, and you laugh at the silly things – until those silly things become the big things that annoy the shit out of you.

Smothering each other in the beginning leads to boredom and lost butterflies because the dopamine hit you give each other wears off. If you're by nature a dopamine chaser, then the crash will happen. You start thinking there's something wrong with the other person or the relationship, mistaking dopamine for love.

I'm guilty of not moving past that point to the 'proper love' bit. I know this isn't the case in all relationships. This is just my experience and the pattern I've followed throughout my life. Maybe some people will find this relatable and think, '*Yes, this is exactly what I do.*' Hopefully, I can share some insight into what I've learned from all the mistakes I feel I've made in the past.

I believe some people are brought into your life for a reason. Whether it's to teach you something or just to give you a great experience, the reasons are endless. My relationship with Dan was my longest relationship to date. We were together for five years, but I think he would even agree it should have ended long before we reached that mark.

As quickly as we fell in love, our relationship followed the same pattern I'd been through before. It became so normalised, so routine. Our favourite part of the day together was dinner on the sofa with a box set. Now, this isn't a bad thing, but I was looking for something more. I didn't even know what it was. I had this fantasy in my head of what love should look and feel like.

I told Dan I didn't believe in marriage, that I just didn't see myself walking down the aisle. But that was a lie. Deep down, I knew I just didn't want to marry him – so he never asked.

Year after year, something was lost between us. Eventually, the arguments became more of a staple in our relationship than the love bit. I became very closed off sexually, just like I had with Ben toward the end. It wasn't fair to Dan. I should have had the balls to let him go.

But we had one beautiful thing that kept us together: a baby. For another three years, I tried. I couldn't see a life without us as a family, but at the same time, I couldn't see a future as one either. Something had to give.

Eventually, I found the courage to end things. Saying goodbye to five years wasn't easy, regardless of how I felt. I did still love him – I just wasn't *in love* with him.

He moved on, and that was that.

CHAPTER 9

Heartbreak, Dates & Single Life

After Dan and I split, it would be six years before I settled again – and boy, did I learn a lot in those years. I had a few fleeting relationships, a couple I thought might go the distance, and a lot of dates! I had a lot of fun, but I also had my heart broken a couple of times along the way.

I don't regret any of the relationships I've had. I call them chapters in the 'Book of Life'. I always joked that one day, I would write a book about my love life and the experiences I've had with different people. However, those men haven't defined me or contributed to who I am; they've just taught me what I didn't want, what I deserved, and where to place my happiness.

The sad thing is, I would let someone take my happiness and my heart and hold it in their hands to either nurture or play with. The men who made my stomach flip ultimately played with my heart and broke it, and the men who wanted to nurture it felt too needy and clingy, so I ran from them.

It's that old saying: 'You always want what you can't have.' The more unobtainable someone or something is, the more you want it. I always felt like if someone didn't want me, there was something wrong with me. And because of that, I wanted that person to like me even more, to validate me.

It's like Simon Cowell. Every contestant on his shows wants to impress him. They don't give a shit about anyone else's opinion or feedback – just Simon's – because he's honest and can hurt people's egos with his bluntness. So, when he does praise someone, their validation is through the roof. There's a bit of neediness in all of us, and we're all craving some form of adoration from another person.

I thought my happiness was someone else's responsibility, that once I found *the one*, all my self-worth would finally be validated. I really hung on to that belief for far too long.

It's so easy to fall into the trap of giving yourself fully to someone – not just sexually, but in other ways. Asking permission, for instance: 'Is it OK with you if I...?' 'Do you mind if I...?' I didn't even realise I was doing it until recently. I still catch myself sometimes, out of habit, and my partner is constantly saying, 'Stop asking for my permission. Do what you want.'

And he's right. When I was asking for permission, it felt like living with a parent again – or like I'd done something wrong and was fearing a telling-off.

The truth is, we both have our own lives and had our own lives before we came together. Who is anyone to tell you what you can and can't do, regardless of your relationship status? If you're committed, the biggest thing is trust. You should trust your partner no matter what. And if that trust is broken – I mean really broken – then that person is not your person.

There was a period a few years ago when I met someone completely out of the blue, and I thought, *This is 'the one.'* When we met, we locked eyes, and neither of us looked away. I had never experienced that before. Usually, when I caught the eye of a cute guy, I'd do that look-away-and-then-look-back thing. But this time felt different. And me being me, believing in the power of the universe, I convinced myself that this man was sent for me.

He wasn't my usual type at all, and I didn't even think I fancied him right away. It felt more like an instant connection. We talked all night, and eventually, he kissed me. And it wasn't just a kiss – it was perfect. He called it *magic*. My head was spinning. I gave him my number and went home on a cloud, telling my friends in the taxi, 'Oh my god, this is it!' Banging on about the universe and the connection I felt.

I'm shaking my head now as I write this because, needless to say, my friends had heard this same speech countless times before. They took my declaration of 'He's the one!' with a pinch of salt.

A couple of days went by and I hadn't heard from him. By that point, I was sure we'd be deep into the WhatsApp relationship hole, but... nothing. Until day three. I was at work, and he called me. I saw his name pop up on my phone, and I nearly threw it across the room – I was in that much shock that he was actually *calling* and not just texting. I gathered my composure, answered in my polite 'telephone voice,' and said, 'Hello?'

The conversation was short and sweet. He asked me out for dinner. Obviously, I said yes. Then, I immediately started planning the wedding. (I joke. But seriously, the butterflies were going nuts.)

I know this is all my own doing. We had a great night together, and then he didn't get in touch. That unconscious feeling of rejection started to creep in, and just as I was about to dismiss it as another failed connection, he appeared – validating my feelings. And so the cycle of torture began. Because with him, that's exactly what it was.

He called me for a start, and straight away, I thought, *This is so different from any man I've dated. He's man enough to just pick up the phone and arrange a date.* The evening of the date, he picked me up – tick. He paid for dinner – tick, tick. And then... I slept with him. Oh shit. Not exactly a tick, but more like, *Oh well.*

When I think I've met someone special, I do like to be traditional and wait to have sex – usually two weeks, max – so I can get to know them better and play a little hard to get. But with him? I had a 'fuck it' moment. Literally.

He wasn't much of a texter, though. So, the next day, when I saw that he hadn't read my message – and then left me on *blue ticked* for hours after he did – I was climbing the walls. Absolutely chastising myself for sleeping with him so soon, my stomach in knots.

I tried distracting myself, but every two minutes, I'd check my phone to see if he'd replied. I called my friend Ross, going over every last detail of the night and overanalysing my text to him, making excuse after excuse for why he hadn't replied. 'He's obviously busy. He has a business to run.'

Then, just as I was about to commit the most desperate act of all – double texting him – he finally replied. And asked me out again.

I spent hours in knots, feeling sick, thinking I wasn't worthy enough or that there was something wrong with me because I wasn't at the forefront of his mind the way he was in mine. And then, with a click of his fingers, he'd take all that away. I was completely spellbound.

I hardly knew this man, yet I allowed myself to feel unworthy. This wasn't his fault at all. He didn't owe me anything. He hadn't promised me anything. He'd set his boundaries straight from the start, saying he wasn't looking for anything serious. And me? I just smiled and replied, 'We'll see.' I ignored his boundaries completely, creating something in my mind that wasn't real.

We kept dating, and eventually, we even committed to being a couple. He told me he loved me fairly early on, and I believed him. But he was still the same when it came to communication – leaving messages unanswered for hours at a time. I spent more days in knots than feeling relaxed.

Our dating was mostly confined to weekends. We'd go out for dinner, then head to his late-night bar, where I'd sit at the end of the counter until closing time, sometimes into the early hours, just waiting for him. Looking back, I wish I'd had the guts to do what I really wanted: to go home, get some sleep, and let him come to mine after cashing up if he wanted to. If he didn't, fine. But no. I stayed, every single time.

I changed who I was at my core for this man. I put him on a pedestal, letting him pick me up and put me down whenever it suited him. I was consumed with being the *perfect girlfriend* – the way I looked, dressed, acted... I had to be perfect, and it was exhausting.

Once again, he never asked this of me. It was all me – how I perceived our relationship, trying to be what I thought he wanted. We rarely argued because I was too busy pleasing him to stand up for myself. But on the rare occasions we did, I'd end up crying and begging him not to leave. So pathetic.

I was never pictured out with him. I wanted to keep our relationship private. Every time I was spotted in Manchester with a man, we'd get papped, and the headlines would spin whatever narrative suited them. I hated it. Sometimes, I was just out with a friend, and suddenly, the papers would be shouting, 'Steph Waring steps out with mystery man!' Everyone had an opinion about my love life, but no one had a clue what was actually going on.

He was a very private man with no social media, and I liked that about him. He wasn't one for selfies or attention-seeking posts. But even with his privacy, I always trusted my gut. And when something bad was about to happen, I could *feel* it – even when everything on the surface seemed perfectly normal. Then, boom – it would hit. My heart ripped out of my chest. Yes, it really is that dramatic.

I've called this event four times in my life. Everything seems fine, I get that strange gut feeling, and then, just like that, a breakup happens.

I did not take this particular breakup well. I went nuclear – a fact my friend Tamara Wall, who plays Grace in *Hollyoaks*, can fully attest to. Two days after he broke it off – over the phone, I might add – I was booked to do *Celebrity Big Brother's Bit on the Side*.

I asked Tam if she wanted to come with me. I was booked into a hotel, and honestly, I needed the company and a distraction. I wiped my tears, painted a smile on my face, and boarded the train to London.

Now, I'm not a big drinker – in fact, I'm terrible at it. I only have to smell a glass of wine, and the room starts spinning. And I am definitely not a day drinker. But Tam? She can drink a bar dry and wake up fresh as a daisy.

She bought a couple of bottles of prosecco for the train journey, and in my attempt to embrace the single, 'I-can-do-whatever-I-want', empowered woman vibe…

I drank! We laughed and laughed on that train, sharing all our relationship crap with each other. Tam made me feel so much better. Luckily, by the time we arrived at Elstree, I wasn't drunk, just a bit tipsy. To be fair, Tam did most of the drinking.

I did my bit on the panel. Callum Best and Bobby Norris were on it too. I love and hate live TV. I always get so nervous, thinking I'll say the wrong thing, not be funny, stumble over my words, or worse. Somehow, I've always managed to blag my way through anything live. After the show, Callum, Tam, and I went for a drink. What started as one drink turned into many, and before we knew it, it was daylight.

We had to get the train back to Manchester with zero sleep. I still don't know how I wasn't throwing up constantly. But, of course, I had dropped the text to my ex while I was pissed. When I didn't hear back, I dropped another. Then another. I was pretty much unstoppable. I'm sure there was even a sobbing voice note thrown in for good measure. I mean, why not? In for a penny, right?

I was crying on the train – loudly, not quietly. So much so that Tam put her headphones on and pretended to be asleep.

At one point, I ended up sitting on the floor in the doorway of the carriage so I could wail without interruption. Oh God, I was a mess. Whenever Tam and I tell this story now, we're hysterical with laughter at how ridiculous the whole thing was. It's honestly one of my favourite stories. I'm convinced that if *How to Lose a Guy in 10 Days* hadn't already been made, I'd have been the inspiration for it. I was definitely the 'what not to do' girl.

Ultimately, it wasn't losing *him* that broke my heart – it was the rejection. Looking back, we barely knew each other. What I mean is he didn't know me *to my core*. It was all very surface-level. And while I was doing my absolute best to be anything but myself, it's no surprise he dumped me.

I can't blame the man for not seeing me as his everything. I just wasn't his person – and that's okay. If I'd known this back then, I definitely would have dialled down the crazy.

I think, in relationships, we put so much pressure on the other person not to break our hearts. I've heard it so many times from friends, too. They'll say to a new potential partner, 'I've been really hurt in the past, so please don't break my heart.' And with that, they've just handed over a grenade. That's exactly what it is because you know that thing's going to blow. You're basically making someone else responsible for protecting your heart – someone you've probably only just met.

Then, when the grenade drops and your heart gets smashed to pieces, you blame that person. You call them every name under the sun because they dared not to love you. 'Urgh, he's such a twat.' 'The bastard.' And so on. Somehow, you go from loving someone so much to hating them in the blink of an eye – all because they didn't want you.

I had a brief relationship once, about six months long (yes, another one). This time, it was me doing the heartbreaking. The guy adored me, but we wanted different things. I could only offer so much, and he wasn't what I was looking for long-term. Even though we got on brilliantly, the arguments came sooner than in any relationship I'd been in. Our communication was off.

I ended it. I didn't cheat. I didn't deliberately do anything to hurt him. But because I didn't want what he was offering, I became, in his mind, the worst person in the world. He blocked me on all social media, and to this day – eight years later – I think I'm still blocked. It's been a while since I've done the old social media stalk, though.

And let's be real, as any woman will tell you, we can be crazy bitches after a breakup. And it's often not the ex you're stalking; it's the new girlfriend. Torturing yourself by checking to see what she has that you didn't. Trying desperately to find something wrong with her, so you can convince yourself he'll see it too – and come running back to you.

When a breakup happens, people's egos get hurt. We take everything so personally, but really, it isn't about us. Taking things personally is one of the most selfish things we can do as humans. For instance, your partner has a bad day at work. They don't want to talk about it, and then *we* automatically assume it's about us. 'What have I done wrong?' 'You're making me feel like shit not answering my calls.' 'Why are you ignoring me?' We make someone else's pain about us.

Then what inevitably happens? The person you're accusing of making you feel like shit because they had a bad day gets defensive, and *then* it does become about you. World War 3 breaks out – for what? Let people have their space. If you know in your heart you haven't done anything to upset your partner or friend, let them have time to deal with whatever it is and just get on with your life. Stop spending all your time wound up because they haven't texted you back within two minutes.

I'm still a work in progress. After the one that broke my heart, I pretty much stayed single for a couple of years. Yes, I dated, but I promised myself I would work on myself and my self-worth and never put someone on a pedestal again. I read all the how-to books: *The Rules, How to Attract Your Soulmate, What Not to Do in Relationships* – you get the picture. I basically put myself through a self-made university course on how to get a man and keep him, while also being an empowered boss bitch whose self-worth is firmly placed on her own pedestal.

I even wrote down a list of qualities I wanted in a man and put it away somewhere. Obviously, this list was too good to be true because, let's face it, no one is perfect – but there's no harm in asking, is there? I decided I would play hard to get, never text back straight away because I was too busy being a boss bitch.

In reality, though, I'm that girl who cannot have one single notification on her phone. It's a weird OCD thing. I really have to try not to look at my phone when a message comes through. And when I've read it? I can't just leave it because my brain goes straight to, 'They know you've read it. They'll think you're rude if you don't reply.' Then I go into assuming-and-fear mode.

So yes, I'm the straight-away replier – or, at most, five minutes. Even if my friends leave me blue-ticked, I automatically assume I've done something wrong.

I'm really trying to learn not to make assumptions and not to take things personally. Like I said, I'm a work in progress. But I *am* getting better. With my current partner, I leave him on blue-ticked all the time, and he does the same with me. And you know what? It really doesn't matter.

So, with the vast trove of knowledge that I had acquired, it was time to put it into action. At the time, I was on a dating site called RAYA. You have to apply to be on it. It's set up for like-minded individuals, mostly in the entertainment industry or similar fields.

I had a few dates from it, but none went anywhere. You could tell the ones that were just on there for a hook-up. I, however, was not into that. I started chatting with a younger guy who used to be a footballer but was now starting his own business in fashion. I don't follow football, so I had no idea who he was – not my usual type – but because Manchester lads were few and far between on RAYA, I clicked 'like,' and we matched.

We messaged back and forth for a bit. The chat was okay, nothing that made me think he was a potential partner. I was just happy being single and 'trying men on', so to speak – to see who fit. He asked me on a date, and I thought, *What the hell? Just go. You've learned by now that you don't have to give him anything, and if you're not having a good time, you can just come home.* I drove so I wouldn't be in a situation where I'd feel pressured to drink.

He gave me the postcode to his house. I picked him up, and we drove to Piccolino's in Knutsford. He was cute. I don't think I fancied him, but I wanted to see what his chat was like. For me, a guy has to have banter and make me laugh – that's high up on my list.

Anyway, we sat down, and halfway through dinner, he said, 'Oh man, I completely forgot – I have to go and get my hair cut.' I was like, '*Erm…* okay.' I was very dubious. Then he says, 'Do you mind driving me?'

I nearly spat my drink out but held it together. I asked where he needed to go, thinking it would be local. He replied, 'It's in Liverpool.' At this point, he nearly got sprayed with another mouthful of drink. 'Liverpool?' I said, trying not to sound like this was completely out of the ordinary.

Liverpool was a 40-minute drive away. Why on earth I didn't just get my ass in the car and go home, I will never know. It went against all my instincts. I thought, *This could be fun – a little adventure to the middle of Liverpool.* I also thought we could probably get to know each other more while he was getting his hair done.

Now, I must explain – his hair is afro and needed special attention. We actually had a good chat on the drive there. But when I pulled up, I went to gather my things, and he got out of the car, turned to me, and said, 'See you in a couple of hours,' then slammed the door shut.

What. The. Actual. Fuck.

I was speechless. And yes, you're probably judging me for this, but I waited. I *fucking* waited. I sat there in the middle of Liverpool on a Thursday night, waiting for this man I barely knew to get his weave done.

When I told my friend this story, she said, 'Who the hell, in the middle of dinner, goes, *Hmm, I need to go and get my haircut?* Steph, are you an Uber driver?'

The good person in me didn't want to leave him stranded. Yes, I know – he could have ordered an Uber. But there I was, seething. I called my best friend, Ross, who was in complete disbelief and told me to leave him there. Looking back, I wish I had.

I called my eldest daughter, who was 14 at the time and told her to text me, saying she needed me to pick her up from her dad's because she wanted to come home.

When he finally got back in the car, I showed him the text. Date over.

I dropped him home – because I'm a decent human being – and then drove myself to Alderley Edge to meet my friend Portia for a drink. And you know what? I had the best night. Just one drink because I was driving.

The guy in question texted me the next day to say he had a good night. I promptly ghosted him. The End.

Before lockdown, I had been single for almost a year, so I went into it with no one to bubble with other than my kids. I know lockdown was extremely hard for some people, and my heart really does go out to the thousands who lost loved ones and their livelihoods. Everyone had different experiences, and I have to say, I loved mine.

Everything just stopped overnight. The relentless train of filming came to a halt, and for the first time in 12 years, I felt free. No alarms to set, no commitments to anyone other than being there for my kids. It was endless home workouts and being introduced to TikTok by my nine-year-old daughter, which quickly became my addiction of 2020.

The sun shone every single day. It felt like Mother Nature had a chance to breathe, and my God, it was the best spring I have ever seen. My daily routine became walking, working out, TikTok, and binge-watching every season ever made of *The Real Housewives*. I think I was the healthiest I'd ever been in both mind and body. Well, I say that, but I've learned a lot more about nutrition since then. At the time, I was still somewhat restrictive with food and had a pretty rigid routine. It suited me, though. I had no one to answer to other than myself.

I didn't drink a drop of alcohol, either. In fact, I hadn't had a drink in about a year at that point.

Of course, I still held onto the dream of meeting someone. In that respect, I was lonely. I was 42 – well past the *Bridget Jones* phase – and I wondered if 'the one' would ever come along for me. I dreamt about him, but he never had a face. I always believed that one day I would get married and finally be happy with my person, but when?

CHAPTER 10

Tom – the Caught Butterfly

*I*t was summer 2015, and I was on a second date with a guy I'd met the previous week. He was 25, covered in tattoos, and honestly, he was either my midlife crisis or a mistake. At the time, I was just having fun. His name was Rick, and the first time we met, we got papped together. Next thing I knew, we were splashed all over the *Daily Mail*. The press somehow found out his name and decided to make up a whole relationship story about us. Apparently, he was a nightclub owner, which was news to me since he was actually a barber who still lived at home with his mum. I'm sure he's moved out by now.

To me, he wasn't anything serious, just a bit of fun. He took me out for a lovely meal and mentioned that we'd been invited to the opening of a nightclub called Suburbia. The owner of Suburbia was Tom Thornton-Brookes. When I was introduced to him, I remember thinking, *I like his name.* He was very handsome and charming, but our meeting was brief because this extremely tall blonde woman came bounding over, holding out her hand, and said, 'Hi, I'm Sarah, his wife.' (She spells it Sarha, but for ease, I'm spelling it how it sounds.)

'Nice to meet you,' I said. We had a quick chat – she was enthusiastic – and then she was off. I saw Tom again later that evening, but just in passing. I certainly wasn't thinking anything untoward. I was happy with my 25-year-old toy. Plus, he was married, and anyone with a ring on their finger was a flat no. It was a great night from what I remember – the music, the vibe – everything was right up my street.

Rick and I went back a couple of weeks later for another night out. This time, I had a brief chat with Tom at the bar when I asked if he had elderflower to go with my prosecco. Of course, he did. That was pretty much it. Not long after, Rick and I fizzled out, and I never went back to Suburbia. I don't even know why. I really liked it.

Fast forward five years to December 2, 2020. I'd just finished a marathon of *The Real Housewives of New York* and was heading to bed. It must've been around 12:30 a.m., and my body clock was still in full lockdown mode; I couldn't fall asleep before midnight. I got into bed and did my usual bedtime scroll through social media: Instagram first, then Facebook.

While I was on Facebook, 'People You May Know' popped up. I scrolled through and saw a familiar name: Tom Thornton-Brookes. I remembered the name more than I remembered him, and for some reason, I hit *Send Friend Request.* I never click that button, but something inside me just said, *Click it.* I put my phone on charge and went to sleep.

The next morning, I woke up to two notifications: *Tom Thornton-Brookes has accepted your friend request,* and *Tom Thornton-Brookes has sent you a message.* Intrigued, I opened it and read:

Good evening, Stephanie.
It's been a long time. How have you been?
x

For a start, the message was sent at 3:50 a.m., so he must've been having a *good* evening. He told me much later that he'd had a few whiskeys at that point and thought I absolutely needed to hear from him right then and there.

I followed up with a reply at a respectable 1:56 p.m., playing hard to get. (I'm joking, of course.) For all I knew, he could've still been married. My gut feeling, though, was that he wasn't. He hadn't confirmed it yet, but our chat was perfectly platonic… until he casually dropped into the conversation a couple of hours later that he was divorced.

I wasn't sure if I fancied him at this point. I just had a vague memory of meeting him all those years ago, and although I remembered him being handsome, I still didn't know. For me, it's all about the connection – getting to know someone in person. Every relationship seems to grow via text these days, but I couldn't gauge anything until we actually met. Our chat was fine, and we messaged back and forth on Facebook for a while before he asked for my number so we could move the conversation to WhatsApp. I think we'd been talking for about a week before he asked me out on a date. I said yes, and we planned to meet on Friday, December 18.

That Monday, I was getting my hair done at Terrence Paul Hairdressers. My stylist, Rachel, knew Tom from when he had his club in Hale, Cheshire, so she was dishing all the details for me. She told me he was a really good catch and funny. Now, I've said before how important being funny is to me, but I was slightly confused because this side of him hadn't come across in our texts. Rachel's confirmation made me feel a bit more excited about the date.

While I was sitting in the salon – which, let's face it, takes hours – I sent him a text. He'd always been good at responding within a decent time frame, but on this particular day, he didn't read my message for hours. Ugh. I could feel the anxiety building as I checked my phone every five minutes to see if the ticks had turned blue. That old, familiar feeling. The stomach flipped because he was suddenly unobtainable.

In the past, I would mistake this feeling for really liking someone, but it's not that. It's the fear of possible rejection when there's even a hint that something might not happen. Eventually, he did read my message and replied, saying he'd been stuck in appointments all day. Instant relief. All that stomach churning for nothing.

Although, I must admit, I kind of like that feeling. It's addictive. The butterflies were in full swing, and I hadn't even spent five minutes in his company. After he replied, I dropped him the most awkward voice note in my highest-pitched telephone voice. Honestly, I have no game. All those books I read were putting me to shame at that moment.

Still, I had every intention of going on the date and being as closed off as possible – almost enigmatic. Don't give too much, don't overshare, make him want to come back for more. Funnily enough, Tom's best friend's advice to him was, 'Don't be you, Tom.'

So, we both had a plan to *not* be ourselves on our first date.

The day arrived. Friday. I was a nervous ball of energy all day, going through the usual get-ready routine. Dinner was at 7:30 p.m., and he was picking me up at 6:45 p.m. He was right on time. He knocked on the door, and when I opened it, I saw him for the first time in five years.

Obviously, I'd stalked his Facebook and gone through every photo on there, but for some reason, Tom looks different in almost every picture, so it was hard to gauge which face would turn up on my doorstep. I was pleasantly surprised. *Handsome* was my first thought. His hair was quite long on top, and he was wearing a suit and holding an umbrella because it was raining. *Tick,* I thought. *He's a gentleman.*

'Hello. Ready to go?' he said, walking me to his car. I was nervous. We were about to drive for 30 minutes to Alderley Edge, where dinner was booked. I'm not great with small talk.

He opened the car door for me, and I got in. *Just breathe. Be cool. Don't be you,* I thought to myself.

When he got in, he said I looked nice, and we set off for dinner. I needed a drink, stat. For someone who hadn't had alcohol in a year, it was definitely needed tonight. I was nervous and just needed to relax. What's the worst that could happen? He doesn't call me again?

We arrived at the restaurant. We had to wear masks, which I hated because I couldn't breathe and felt my makeup sweating off my face. Luckily, we didn't have to wear them while sitting at the table.

As we sat down and I had my first glass of prosecco, I don't know what happened, but the pair of us did not stop talking. Every barrier I had up came down almost straight away, as did his. We talked about everything, and I mean *everything*. I told him things on that first date I had never even said out loud to another person. I guess I just thought, *If he doesn't like me for me, for who I really am, then this isn't meant for me.* I didn't want to play games anymore. The men I've dated in the past, the ones I hadn't been myself with, didn't deserve the real me.

Tom was a gentleman, and there was something about him that was different from what I'd experienced before. He was a man. Although, as I got to know him better, I've definitely questioned his maturity at times. After dinner, he drove me home, and I asked him in. I didn't want the date to be over, and, to be honest, I was a bit pissed, so I thought, *Why not?* He came in and sat on my sofa while I poured myself a white Zinfandel rosé – classy, I know.

We talked for a bit, and I could sense the gentleman in him was going to leave me with just a kiss on the cheek. So, mid-conversation, I looked at him and said, 'Are you going to kiss me or what?' I think he was taken aback by my bluntness – a trait he now says is one of my best qualities. He kissed me, and it was a *good* kiss. I just needed to know if the chemistry was there. We had the chat down; now it was all riding on the kiss.

After that kiss, I felt something – the butterflies – and this time, it wasn't because of any game playing or fear of rejection. There was something very honest about us.

After Tom left, he texted me:

'I had a really good time. Thank you. Didn't expect to come away smiling like this. P.S. You're a really good kisser.'

I responded with, *'Me too. You're definitely a nice surprise. Looking forward to seeing you again. x'*

He replied, *'We'll have to get the second date booked in sooner rather than later. x'*

This was new to me.

Usually, I had to wait at least a couple of days before the subject of a second date even came up. And here was a man who wanted to see me the very next night. *Oh my God, what is happening?* He wanted to cook me dinner at my house the following evening. So much for my *I'm going to take this one slow* attitude.

The second date was amazing. He cooked me steak, and the red wine flowed. Once again, we talked for hours and snogged each other's faces off like we were teenagers. Dinner over my dining room table immediately became our favourite thing.

As soon as our dating journey began, another lockdown was put in place, which meant dining out was no longer an option. In a way, I'm thankful for that because I don't think we would've had the same dating experience. This was completely out of the ordinary, and I wasn't conforming to any of my usual patterns.

After the second date, the third followed the very next day – Sunday. He invited me over to his place in Macclesfield, offered to cook again, and suggested we chill and watch a movie. I was slightly hungover (the third glass of red is never a good idea), and being new to drinking again, my body was not used to it. But I didn't want to say no. I wanted to carry on this whirlwind of new butterflies I was feeling, so I sucked it up and said yes.

When I arrived, I met his two little dogs, Daisy and Lola. Straight away, I knew I was going to have to put in more effort and groundwork with Lola than I did with Tom. She was his baby and only had eyes for him. Daisy, however, was all over me as soon as I walked through the door.

We had dinner and got comfy on the sofa while deciding on a movie. After a weekend of getting to know each other, I needed this – a bit of quiet time. Now came the real test: silence for a couple of hours.

As I lay in his arms watching some rubbish comedy film, I didn't know it at the time, but Tom tells me that's when he knew he loved me. After only three days, he said he was holding me and thought, *Fuck, this feels different.* That's when he knew he was in trouble, that this was going to be something special, and that he was quickly falling.

What can I say? I had him at hello.

There was one thing about being with Tom I hadn't felt before in any relationship: I could 100% be my authentic self. He loves every single bit of me, the good and the bad – even though he would argue and say there are no bad bits, just challenges. I knew this early on, like the first time he FaceTimed me. I have *never* FaceTimed any man before. I almost ignored his call, but then I thought, *Fuck it, he sees me as I am all the time; I'm sure he can deal with FaceTime me.* What I didn't realise is that I'm the only one judging myself when I see my reflection glaring back at me, all imperfect. Now I FaceTime him looking all kinds of states. No makeup, spots, hungover, bedhead – you name it, he's seen it. And for some weird reason, he finds me more beautiful without makeup on. In past relationships, I would either sleep in my makeup or get up early to at least put some concealer on. Obviously, I didn't do this in my long-term relationships, but I never felt comfortable enough to just be me until Tom.

He doesn't scare easily, put it that way. One of the things he loves most about me is my bluntness. He'd argue that past men must've been a little sensitive or just couldn't handle it, whereas he finds it humorous and endearing. I think if you're not compatible with someone and they don't get your banter or humour, it just causes misunderstandings and arguments. I used to constantly say, 'I didn't mean it like that.' Tom understands my thought process and knows I'm not being a bitch – my delivery is just very blunt.

As I got to know Tom, I quickly realised that his texting personality is completely different from who he actually is as a person. One word: BIG KID. Yes, the man is playful and fun with a big heart and makes me laugh like no one else ever has. His humour would probably get him cancelled these days, and I'm constantly saying, 'TOM!!!' while laughing and shaking my head. I love being around him. I feel like a big kid myself when I'm with him, just having fun with my best friend – and also fancying him like mad.

Like I said, our dating pretty much happened over my dining room table, and as that developed, so did my love for red wine. I had always loved a red, but my palate only stretched from a Rioja to a Malbec. Now, with Tom's influence and his love of reds, my favourite is a Passimiento. Instead of box sets, we'd eat dinner at the table, play cards, listen to music, and talk for hours. We did this for almost three years. We were constantly learning about each other, and our communication was on point – although, let's be honest, this massively needed work during our second year together. You think you have great communication until the arguments start, and they inevitably do. At this point, you stop listening to each other and become obsessed with being right.

At the time of writing this, we've been together for three and a half years, and we still don't live together. However, he's moving in at the beginning of next month, which is just three weeks away. Let's get into *why* it's taken this long. As our relationship quickly developed, there was one thing that slowed it down for the better, and had it not been for this, I probably would have fallen into my old pattern of moving in too quickly and then facing a foreseeable breakup. Not living together gave us time, space, and growth.

The first sleepover did not go well for me. I've never been the best sleeper and have dealt with insomnia in the past, but only on the occasional night – nothing that ever worried me. I've always been fine sleeping next to someone, so it never occurred to me that I wouldn't be this time. However, the first night he stayed over, I could *not* fall asleep. I felt so bad tossing and turning, getting frustrated with myself. By 3 a.m., I ended up sleeping in my daughter's room (she was at her dad's), and I finally fell asleep. I woke up the next day feeling like shit but treated it as a one-off. It wasn't a one-off.

Coupled with the fact that Tom sleeps with his dogs, this was a huge no for me. It's bad enough listening to a grown man snore next to me, never mind two dogs who are louder than him. So, the best thing that's ever happened to me in a relationship? Separate bedrooms.

Honestly, *best thing ever.* Even though the insomnia was bad for a while, separate sleeping spaces are a godsend. We both get our own space and wake up fresh in the morning without the need to punch each other in the face because one of us hogged the bed or snored too loud. You get the point. So now, I'm having an extension built with an extra room so he can finally move in. And with the extension, our dining room table has temporarily become the stand for the TV, so dinners are now in front of the telly with a movie or box set. I cannot wait for our new big kitchen so we can finally get back to dining, talking, and playing cards again. But I'm getting ahead of myself.

The first year was fun. We very quickly became each other's person, each other's plus-one, and not living together was great because we missed each other even though we pretty much spent all our free time together. I knew early on he was going to be my husband. After all the years of relationships and dating and not finding the right one, I just knew Tom was my one. I honestly can't imagine him not being in my life. Before, I'd flip my stomach if my partner hadn't replied to a message or called me. Now, if Tom doesn't reply or leaves me on blue ticks, I know there's a reason, and not one bit of me flips out. He doesn't make me feel unworthy. He constantly reminds me that I'm the best thing that's ever happened to him. He also made it pretty clear early on that I was going to be his wife one day – a topic that made me nervous every time it came up. He could see that I was scared. I don't take marriage lightly because I've waited for the right person. Even though I knew it was Tom, I was still holding something back.

As we approached the end of 2021, we both got COVID. We were holed up in his flat, isolating for 10 days. If that isn't the ultimate relationship test, I don't know what is. Surprisingly, we had the best time even though we were so ill. He actually watched all six seasons of *Sex and the City* and the movies! He loved it, although he still hates Carrie for cheating on Aiden with Big and hasn't gotten over it.

Once we finished isolating, it was the beginning of December, and our anniversary was just a couple of weeks away. I was still feeling rough from COVID, but he had it all planned. I had no idea what we were doing, only that we were going away for the night. The morning of our anniversary, I woke up feeling dreadful – like I had COVID all over again. I needed to shake this off, so I sucked it up, got showered, and made myself up for the day. I'd been so excited to celebrate, and I had a feeling he was going to pop the question. I didn't want to spoil the day by moaning about being ill. That didn't last long. I can't help it; I'm a *say how you feel* kind of girl. My inner monologue has the biggest microphone and zero filter. Anyway, he got the memo: *Steph is not feeling well!*

As we made our way, it became clear he was taking me to the Lake District. We pulled up at a beautiful hotel by Lake Windermere. We weren't staying there, though – this was just Part One of our anniversary day. He'd arranged for us to have afternoon tea and prosecco in the restaurant overlooking the garden and the lake. Unfortunately, it was foggy, so we could only barely see the garden – never mind the lake.

After we'd eaten our crustless sandwiches and jam-filled scones, he took my hand and led me into the garden. I thought, *Oh my God, this is it. He's going to propose.* He stopped and looked out, only to notice there was a main road between the lake and the hotel. A look of confusion spread across his face while my heart was pounding out of my chest, waiting for him to drop to one knee. Then he grabbed my hand and said, 'I'm not feeling this. Shall we go to the hotel?' At this point, I didn't know what was going on, so I just agreed. Maybe this wasn't his plan.

When we got back in the car, he told me the hotel we were staying at was another hour away. I took it in stride – surely, he had a plan. We arrived in Cockermouth. Yes, Cockermouth. And it gets better: the hotel he booked was called The Tithe Barn, which I now lovingly refer to as 'The Titty Barn'. Juvenile, I know. We checked in and made our way to the room. As Tom opened the door and held it for me, right in my eyeline was a bottle of champagne and a card that read '*Congratulations on your engagement*'.

Oh fuck, I thought as I swerved past it straight into the bathroom, pretending I hadn't seen it. In the bathroom, I was feeling two emotions: one of complete joy and happiness because my life was about to change, and another of feeling like I'd been robbed of the surprise. I opened the bathroom door and asked him if he wanted to open the gift I'd brought for him. I'd made a placard of photos from our first year together. He loved it. Then he handed me his gift. It was similar to mine, but in a photo album, with captions under each picture telling the story of our relationship so far.

As I got to the end, there was a picture of a ring. The next page said, *'And did she say yes?'* I turned to him, and he got down on one knee with a small box in his hand. As he opened it, there sat the ring from the photo. He asked me to be his wife. At that moment, it didn't matter how, when, or where he did it. I was flooded with emotion as he took my left hand, and I said yes. He put the ring on and kissed me. I was engaged.

I didn't tell Tom that I'd seen the congratulations note. I didn't want to take away any of the shine from the moment. However, I did eventually tell him earlier this year. We have an honesty in our relationship that's so strong it holds us together, and this wasn't something I wanted to keep from him. It would have been a secret, and I don't have any secrets from Tom. He knows everything about me – although I do occasionally surprise him with stories from my past that spin his head. In a good way, though.

There's nothing I can say about myself or my past that will ever shock him. My past, with all of its experiences, the good and the bad, is what makes me *me*. He's never once judged anything I've done or any relationship I've had. He's that secure in himself, and I trust that whatever I tell him won't ever be met with anger or insecurity. Even when I told him about the note, he just took it in his stride. It wasn't anyone's fault, and like I said, it didn't take anything away from the moment.

So here I am, only a year after meeting this man, engaged to be married. We haven't planned the wedding yet. When he moves in, that'll be the real test for our relationship – being in each other's space full-time. I think it's important for us to spend some time getting to know each other that way before we exchange vows. We've discussed what we want, though I keep changing my mind.

I love the idea of walking down the aisle with all my family and friends there because it's the tradition, and it's how I always thought it would be. But part of me just wants to elope and make it just the two of us somewhere abroad. Then I think of my mum, my dad, and my girls missing out on my big day. We've even talked about doing it in our favourite restaurant, The Coast in Prestbury – a small gathering during the day with around 60 guests, and then an open-invite party in the evening. It makes me smile just thinking about it.

Everything I've said here probably sounds like I have the perfect relationship and that I've finally got it all figured out. I don't. We're a work in progress. We had a rough second year. I'm still not sure how we survived it – There is no handbook, you just have to keep showing up for each other every day, no matter what.

The 'Stephanie' I am in this relationship is the example I want to set for my girls. They are of dating age now, and it scares the life out of me that they might do what I did for the last 30-odd years – not knowing their self-worth. Of course, they will make mistakes, go out with the bad boy, get their hearts broken, and I will be consoling them, telling them, 'He's not good enough for you' and 'You're better off without him'. But I hope that I have finally given them a good example of what they deserve and what real love looks like.

PART FOUR

Unconditionally Mine

CHAPTER 11

The Wonder of Woman

*I*n my eyes, all mothers are superheroes – deep within us lies our very own Wonder Woman. There was a time when having a child might not have happened for me. When I was anorexic all those years ago, I didn't have a period for five years. My reproductive system had completely shut down, and I thought I'd have to come to terms with never being able to conceive. I was crushed at the thought of never knowing what it would be like to be a mother, to create a new life, and feel that unconditional love I so desperately craved.

As I began to put on weight, feeding my monster, my period showed up one day out of the blue when I was 19. I remember feeling so much relief that my body was working the way it should as a woman. Suddenly, there was hope that one day I could have a family of my own. While I was ambitious about building my career as an actress, the thought of having a child wasn't exactly front and centre in my mind. But deep down, I knew it was something I wanted. I'd always wonder, *What would my kids be like? Would they look like me? What kind of impact would they have on the world?*

When I was a child, I played with dolls, pushed a pram around, and pretended to be a mummy. Thinking about that now, it's so odd how we almost groom our daughters from birth to become mothers.

When I fell pregnant with my first child, Mia, I was 27. It was a shock, to say the least, but every part of me wanted that baby. There wasn't a single thought in my head that said I wasn't ready. It was 2004, I was in a relationship with Daniel, and I felt like I was doing well in my career, landing roles and feeling like there was space in my life to become a mother.

But let me tell you – I *hated* being pregnant. Oh my God, did I hate it! I was never actually sick, but I felt sick all day long. I hated the weight gain. I was tired all the time. I just never felt comfortable in my skin. Oh, and no one tells you about the giant piles you get. When all you want to do is sit down – which is pretty much all the time – you have to use a rubber ring because the pain is enough to make you call 999. And trapped wind? That's another one. Towards the end of my pregnancy, I thought I was going into labour. Nope, I just needed to let out a massive fart.

I didn't find out the sex of either of my children. That was one thing I wanted to wait for – the surprise of hearing, 'It's a girl!' or 'It's a boy!' I mean, I'd been growing a baby for nine months. I wanted something to look forward to.

I remember so clearly the day I went into labour. Daniel was on duty at work as a police officer, and it was about 9 a.m. I noticed a small puddle on the bathroom floor that definitely wasn't pee. Now, as a first-time mum, no one can truly prepare you for what labour will be like. You can read all the books in the world, write the most detailed birth plan with whale music, and practice deep breathing for hours at antenatal classes. (Not that I went to antenatal classes, but plenty of women do.)

I'm telling you now, all that goes out the window – maybe not with the first few contractions, depending on how far along you are – but from that first little break of water, my God, the pain hit me in the abdomen like a thunderbolt. 'This is it.' I called Daniel, and he rushed home and drove me to the hospital. The contractions were about 10 minutes apart,

I think – not too close, but each one was getting more painful. When I arrived at the hospital, they examined me, and to my surprise, I was only *1 cm dilated*! '1 cm?' What the actual fuck? They were about to send me home, but then my water broke a bit more, and unfortunately, it had meconium in it – which meant my baby had pooped in the uterus. It was potentially harmful, so I had to stay in the hospital, wired up to a machine so they could monitor the baby. However, this also meant intense pain and no drugs! I needed at least some gas and air; I didn't even get a big inflatable ball to bounce on.

Hours went by, and my stupid uterus did not like dilating at all. The pain was so intense I didn't want anyone near me. If Daniel so much as *tried* to hold my hand, I just gave him *that* look – and so many men know that look.

Finally, it was time: 9 cm, and I was wheeled into delivery. It was time to push, but more importantly, I was given gas and air. At that point, it was a welcome relief, albeit a slight one. I think I'd been in the hospital for around eight hours before I was ready to deliver. I didn't want an epidural, but the pain of pushing was too much. Every time her head came out a little, it would go back in. They offered me an epidural because I was in so much pain, but for some reason, they couldn't get the cannula into my hand. They said if I didn't have the epidural, I'd likely have the baby before midnight, so I opted to just crack on.

But a little while later, they said, 'Oh, we need to cut you now.'

'Er, what the fuck? Cut me?'

'Yes, the baby's head isn't coming out. It's either that or you'll tear.'

Luckily, the anaesthetic kicked in pretty quickly, and the nurse got the scissors out and snipped away.

Just a brief pause to say to any men reading this: yes, this is what us superwomen do to bring a life into the world. Our bodies have war stories –

all the scars, stretch marks, and cellulite – and we are proud because we made a human.

Not long after the snip – an *episiotomy*, to use its technical term, one I hoped I'd never hear again (spoiler: I did) – that one final push, and my baby was here. The nurses placed my newborn on my chest. I was so bewildered, staring at this tiny human that had just come out of me, I completely forgot to ask what sex the baby was.

'It's a girl.'

Well, wow, what a feeling. I know tradition has been thrown out the window these days with gender reveal parties, but I wanted that surprise at the end, and she was so worth the wait. I handed her over to her dad, Daniel. He took her in his arms, and that was it – love at first sight. She looked just like him when she was born. There's no mistaking it; she's a Jillings.

The midwives asked, 'What are you calling her?' And although we hadn't *quite* settled on a name, I knew it was Mia Grace.

As we took Mia home, I wondered where my 'How to Be a Parent' handbook was. Do they not hand them out at the hospital? Does it not just arrive the next day in the post, like an Amazon delivery? Nope, there's no handbook. You can read all the books in the world on how to be the perfect parent – how to get them to sleep, how to get them to eat – but every single baby that's born is unique, with their own little personalities we're yet to see.

Of course, you learn the basics pretty quickly, but one thing I was never, *ever* told about – and I still find it hard to believe no one talks about it – is *THE WINDING*. Oh my God, the winding! I would spend half the night awake after feeding, just praying to get the wind up quickly so she'd fall back to sleep straight away. And just when you think you've got all the wind out, you hear that dreaded noise of the uncomfortable cry. Honestly, for me, the winding was by far the most challenging part.

Well, that's a lie, but I'll get to that later. I navigated being a mum in the only way I knew how – routine. As long as I had the routine down, my baby would fall in line and do what I wanted her to do, which was sleep at 7 p.m. and wake up at 7 a.m. Ideally. Babies love routine – the repetition, the habit of doing something over and over. It breeds familiarity, and they feel comfortable knowing they're safe because they instinctively know what's coming.

I would feed her every four hours. Then bedtime would be bath, bottle, and bed. I did breastfeed in the beginning, but I found it so hard to keep up with Mia. She was using my breast as a pacifier for comfort and wouldn't unlatch, so I never knew if she was getting enough or when she had finished. When I put her on formula, I found it incredibly frustrating when Mia wouldn't drink much – sometimes no more than two ounces. She would just cry at the bottle, and other times, the only way I could get the bottle in her mouth was to put her in her car seat when she was almost asleep, then slip the bottle in. There had to be silence – any distraction and she wouldn't entertain it, even though I knew she was hungry.

It got to the point where I had such bad anxiety around feeding times that I'd sometimes end up in tears when she'd only had a couple of ounces of milk. The books said she should be having at least seven or eight! I felt like such a failure. I remember calling NHS 111 on Christmas Day 2005 because of this very problem. There *must* be something wrong with her. I spiralled into the depths of despair, fearing the worst – that something was wrong with my baby.

With Mia, the anxiety came more from her not doing what I thought she should be doing and the endless stream of information from books and internet mums. I put all this pressure on my tiny human to be something she wasn't. She wasn't a fussy eater – she just had a mother who needed to be in control. I promised myself I'd never fall into the same trap again if I had another baby. I'd let my baby lead me. And that last sentence? A big, fat lie.

Once we got past the baby stage, I found myself a single mother of one. As I said in the previous chapter, Daniel and I were more friends than anything, and we didn't have the foundation to grow on as a family.

Being a single mother – at least from what I can remember when Mia was a toddler and before I went back to *Hollyoaks* – I absolutely loved it. We had a little flat, just the two of us. She spent a lot of time with her dad, and we eventually split our time with Mia 50/50 – one week on, one week off – which worked for us and still does to this day.

Mia was a well-behaved child, so I never dealt with tantrums or felt like I was tearing my hair out. We just had fun together. Money was tight, but I budgeted carefully. I never felt like we went without. I pretty much walked everywhere with her in her buggy, and when I needed the internet, which wasn't often back in 2007, as I wasn't as glued to it as I am now, I'd just walk to the local library, check my emails and Facebook every other day, and that was that.

Life was simple then. Not long after, I got *that* call to go back to *Hollyoaks*. That call changed everything for me and Mia. This time, I was determined to do it right: save my money, and invest in property. I had no idea I'd end up staying there for 16 years, but early on, I made sure to be smart with my finances. As soon as I started earning, I put money away.

I saved enough to buy my first house in 2008, and then in 2011, I bought my second. I still live here to this day with Mia and another little arrival in 2010 that once again changed my life.

CHAPTER 12

Mother Interrupted

$\mathcal{I}$ had been in a relationship with Dan for about a year. I was 31, almost 32, and I don't know where it came from, but something inside me just made me say these words while we were sitting on the sofa one night watching TV. I looked at Dan and said, 'Do you want to have a baby?' There was no hesitation from him, and that was it. I don't know how this idea of a baby came about for me. I wasn't yearning for another child, but I just felt this pull inside me, so I went with it. I guess I was just in tune with what was ahead for me.

I was settled at *Hollyoaks*, I had bought my first house, Dan had moved in, and he was great with Mia. I felt like I had it all. I knew Dan would be an amazing father, so I just went with my gut. As soon as I said it, I knew it was the best decision I'd ever made. I didn't look back once. I just remember having this constant feeling of excitement.

We started trying right away and fell pregnant almost as soon. My period was late, so I excitedly bought a pregnancy test, did my thing, and we waited for the blue line to pop up. I'm old school. I didn't like the idea of a digital stick telling me if I was pregnant or not. I wanted the double-blue line. Sure enough, I didn't even have to wait a minute; that line was bright blue. I was pregnant!

I had only been back at *Hollyoaks* for a year and was terrified of losing my job because I knew I'd have to be written out for maternity leave. So, stupidly, because I was a natural people pleaser, I went in to tell the bosses that I was pregnant. They were really thrilled for me, and I told them I was due in September 2010. Then I followed it up by saying I'd be back to work after the Christmas break.

What on earth was I thinking? Honestly, back then, I didn't know my value, and I put the fear of losing my job ahead of my own well-being and time with my new baby. This agreement only gave me four months off work. The actresses who've had babies on the show since then have taken the full year, with their jobs waiting for them as soon as their maternity leave was up. When I look back, I now know there was a reason I needed to be back in Cindy's shoes sooner rather than later.

The day we had our first scan was my 32nd birthday. What an amazing present: to see my baby and hear the heartbeat for the first time. I know it was too early to know the sex, but Dan and I agreed we didn't want to find out and would wait until the birth, just like I did with Mia.

Again, I hated being pregnant. I was hoping the second time around would be different, but nope. Those first few weeks of constant nausea without actually being sick, going off my favourite foods, my body growing at a rapid rate – my belly popped pretty much straight away. I remember being on set around 12 weeks, and one of the actors said to me in a cutesy, slightly patronising voice, 'Aw, even your little legs are getting chubby.'

I was mortified. With all my eating issues – and still battling bulimia intermittently (though not while I was pregnant) – I still had the devil on my shoulder. That one comment sent me into a spiral that was hard to come back from. The actor, to this day, has no idea what he said or what he did, and that's okay because it wasn't out of malice or to hurt me. It was just an observation, and he was being silly. But I took that comment and wore it like a coat with pins in it. It fucking hurt.

Working while being heavily pregnant, especially at the height of summer, was not fun. I probably wasn't much fun to be around, either. If I'm thinking it, I'm more than likely saying it. I am working on this and trying to fix the filter between my mind and my mouth. So, if I felt uncomfortable or too hot, *everybody* would know about it.

My storyline on the show to write me out for maternity leave didn't involve Cindy, my character, being pregnant, so hiding the bump was an art form in itself. I was constantly behind something – a counter, a cushion – but the main prop I had was a massive bag. I mean, every time I was on screen, I looked like I was packed for a week's holiday! However, the pièce de résistance of hiding the bump was Cindy's wedding day when she was marrying a 75-year-old millionaire – of course. The bouquet of flowers to cover my bump was ginormous, absolutely huge, but very Cindy.

Every Friday, Dan and I would have a Nando's. For anyone who doesn't know, Nando's is a chicken restaurant that made the term 'Peri-Peri' roll off everyone's lips. This was back when Nando's blew up out of nowhere, even though they'd been around for at least 10 years prior. Suddenly, everyone was having one, and even some of the cast were given a black card, which meant they could flash this card and have as much free chicken as they wanted. I *wanted* one of these cards.

I was obsessed, although even now, I still order the same thing: 'double chicken wrap with peri tamer, corn on the cob, and peri-peri chips.' I don't think Nando's today is what it once was. Its time has definitely passed. Now, it feels like they're just churning out meals, which seem to have shrunk while the prices have shot up. I remember it being so much cheaper and better value for money.

Anyway, when I was pregnant, I was introduced to Nando's, and that was it. That was my treat meal every Friday, followed by a bag of Maltesers and an episode of *24*! Still feeding my Jack Bauer obsession. It got to the point where, towards the end, I was counting down my pregnancy in Nando's: 'Just seven to go.' Seven Nando's doesn't sound like much compared to seven weeks!

It was Wednesday night, September 15, 2010, and something in my gut said to Dan, 'Let's go for a Nando's.' At the time, I didn't know I wasn't going to make it to our usual Friday night treat. It was just a normal Wednesday night, with about a week to go until my due date.

The next day, I started having dull, period-like pains. They began in the morning and came and went throughout the day, but I didn't think I was in labour because the pain wasn't intense – not like it was with Mia. I carried on with my day, but by dinner time, the pains had become more frequent. That's when I thought, *Maybe this is it.*

We called the hospital, but they said not to come in yet as my water hadn't broken and my contractions weren't close enough. So, we had dinner – a curry, one of those foods on the 'induce labour' list – and went for a walk afterwards because that's also supposed to help move things along.

After the walk, the pains – let's give them their actual name, contractions – started to get closer and a lot more painful. Still, it wasn't yet at the *Give me the epidural now!* stage. We called the hospital again and were advised to come in, so I called my mum to look after Mia.

I had planned on having a water birth because, from what I remembered, being on dry land last time was not fun at all. I also wanted to see if I could have this baby without an epidural, just like I did with Mia. I don't know if it was an ego thing, but there is something so primal about giving birth. All my natural instincts kicked in. I believed I could push this baby out, feeling every single inch of pain rip through my body, and then stand proudly, hands on my hips, just like Wonder Woman.

In this fantasy, I'm even wearing a cape.

When we arrived at the hospital, I was checked to see how far along I was. Based on previous experience, I wasn't expecting much, maybe 3 cm dilated at best, followed by being sent to a ward to wait with no gas and air – just a big inflatable ball to bounce on. Honestly, who came up with that idea? Nice try, but no thanks.

This time, though, those magic words fell on my ears: 'You're 7.5 cm dilated. Let's take you down to the birthing suite.' I was in shock, to say the least. Before I knew it, I was wheeled straight to the birthing pool and handed gas and air. The room was lovely – there was a little kitchen, a TV, a sofa, and a giant pool. Okay, maybe not *giant*, but it was a big oval bath.

I quickly got into my birthing attire – a vest – and slid into the pool, clutching my new best friend, the gas and air canister. Dan and I even had a laugh trying it out before the midwife arrived. The contractions were strong but manageable, and Dan put the TV on for some background distraction. I remember *Friends* playing, though just to clarify, he wasn't sitting there glued to Ross and Rachel while I was in the middle of labour. It was just there, buzzing away in the background.

For a moment, I thought, *Wow, this whole giving birth thing is a piece of cake the second time around.* But then it happened – I felt a pop. My water had broken. And the moment that happened, the pain shot through my body like a lightning bolt. The noise I made? I'm pretty sure only wild dogs could hear it. 'Oh, Fuck' Yep, there it was. LABOUR. I hadn't escaped anything after all.

At this point, the gas and air became more of a comfort prop than an actual help. I was sucking on it every few seconds, but it just felt like plain air. Then, the need to push hit me like a freight train.

Before I ever gave birth, I used to wonder what 'the need to push' felt like and how I'd know when it was time. Let me tell you: you *know*. Your body has this incredible, almost primal way of taking over, and every mother who's had a vaginal birth without heavy pain relief will tell you – it feels like you need to have the biggest poop of your life. Yes, that unmistakable '*It's happening, whether I'm on a toilet or not*' feeling.

Now imagine that sensation cranked up to 100. You'd think pushing would be the easy part – just a couple of pushes and out comes the baby, right? Nope. When you feel that overwhelming urge to push, coupled with a contraction giving you a not-so-gentle nudge, it's like running a marathon. After one push, you think, *Surely the head's out now?* But no. The head comes out a little, then slides right back in. You would have thought that after having Mia, this experience would be ingrained in my memory. It's weird how you just casually forget what the most excruciating pain of your life feels like. I think if we did, no woman would voluntarily be up for doing it again... and again.

Of course, every labour is different. To all those mothers out there who claim it was just one push and their baby popped out – or to the ones who didn't even know they were pregnant – I envy you. You clearly have a very gifted vagina.

So, there I was, floating in the pool, the midwife encouraging me with every contraction and Dan behind me, being the most supportive cheerleader. It was around 10:45 p.m., and all I could think was, *Push as hard as you can. Get the head out. Have this baby before midnight. Once the head's out, it's plain sailing.*

Also, the midwife mentioned those words: '*If the head doesn't come out soon, we may need to do an episiotomy.*' *Hell no*, I thought. With the next contraction, I pushed, yelled, screamed, and felt like my head was going to explode. And there it was—my baby's face. I could see it between my legs, through the water. It was the most surreal moment. I recognised that face – it was *my* face, the one I remembered from my own baby pictures. The connection was instant.

The next contraction came, and I pushed with everything I had. This time, I felt another pop, and this one didn't feel good. At that moment, I had no idea what it was – my adrenaline was entirely focused on giving birth. I scooped my baby up from the water and onto my chest, mesmerised, just staring at her little face. I was bewildered by how much I could see myself in her.

Once again, the midwife asked, 'What is it?'

I forgot to look. AGAIN.

So, I looked down. 'It's a girl,' I said, and then repeated it over and over, almost questioning myself. 'It's a girl? It's a girl? It's a girl?' I had been so sure I was having a boy. But honestly, I didn't care. I was completely in love. I couldn't stop staring at her.

Dan cut the cord, and I handed her over so he could hold his daughter for the first time. Meanwhile, the midwife helped me out of the pool and onto the nearby bed – it was time to deliver the placenta. *Shit, I forgot about that part,* I thought.

'You'll feel another contraction,' the midwife said.

Another one? I thought I was done! Baby's out!

The contraction came, and honestly, it wasn't too bad, considering I'd just pushed out a seven-pound human. And there it was – the placenta, the organ that had been my baby's lifeline for nine months. It's not the most pleasant thing to look at. I know some mothers use their placenta for medicinal purposes – I've yet to research the benefits of ingesting it. Honestly, the thought makes me a little queasy. But then again, the idea of it just being tossed in the trash feels strange, too.

Anyway, onto the bad news. In my haste to get the baby out and avoid an episiotomy – which I did – *that* pop I felt turned out to be a big tear along my vaginal wall. *Lovely.* So, I didn't escape anything after all.

If I'd had the episiotomy, it would've been a neat cut, easy to stitch, with no scarring, and it probably would've healed faster. But with a tear, the stitching took ages. My insides were all over the place, and the midwife had to piece them back together. She didn't do a great job, though – years later, I still had this little extra bit of skin flapping around down there. Okay, I'm exaggerating, but it was noticeable. Eventually, I had it removed and also went for a rejuvenation. Honestly, as a woman, I can say it's the best money I've ever spent.

After I was stitched up, I had my daughter lying on my chest. We already had her name picked out: **Lexi Grace.** At the time, I was obsessed with *Grey's Anatomy* and loved the character Lexie Grey. One day, when I was thinking of names, I suggested it to Dan: *'What about Lexi Grace?'* The *Grace* was a nod to her sister, Mia – they share the same middle name. Since they don't share the same dad, I wanted them to have something meaningful in common.

Lexi Grace Waring Hooper was born on September 16, 2010, at 11:13 p.m.

This time, there was no overnight stay in the hospital. With Mia, I stayed until the morning, but this time, we were sent home pretty much as soon as all the paperwork was done. Honestly, I couldn't wait to get her home and for her to meet her sister.

They say the definition of madness is doing the same thing over and over and expecting a different outcome. After everything I went through with Mia and my obsession with her feeding and routines, I told myself, *This time, it will be different. I'll be so chill. I'll just be led by my baby.*

Did that happen? Absolutely not.

In fact, I was so far gone that the weekend before I was due to return to *Hollyoaks* after the Christmas break in 2011 (yes, that God-awful decision to sign away being at home with my baby so I could slip back into Cindy's heels and strut onto the set for fear of losing my job), I ended up in the back of an ambulance, being mentally assessed at the hospital. It was the worst time of my life – or at least that's how it felt.

I *should* have been in the throes of motherhood, glowing, breathing in every single moment with her. But I wasn't. A few years later, I spoke about my experience with postnatal depression in a magazine. Let me tell you now – I did not have postnatal depression. It was just the only label I could attach to what had happened to me.

I can't roll back the clock or change anything, but I know this: I was out of control. I was not okay.

When you've learned a behaviour, your body remembers it. You're so hardwired to it that you unconsciously repeat it without even realising. For me, the emotions were rooted in anxiety – an anxiety born from control. That need to control was ingrained in me years before, during my battle with anorexia. Back then, the only thing I felt I *could* control was what I ate and how my body looked.

When I had Mia, that need for control shifted. I wanted to sleep train her and feed her at set times of the day – not because it was best for her, but because it suited what I *needed*. I needed my baby to sleep. I was terrified I'd have one of those babies who never slept, the ones that keep you awake all night screaming.

When I was pregnant with Mia, I'd heard so many horror stories, and there were endless books about sleep training – let them cry it out, co-sleep, don't co-sleep, put them on a schedule. The conflicting advice from books and mum forums only added to my fear. But as it turned out, I didn't need to worry.

Mia slept through the night from 12 weeks old. She was an amazing sleeper.

But, of course, I didn't let it go. I switched my obsession to her feeding. The books told me how much she *should* be drinking, and the forums had a thousand different opinions. The truth was, Mia was never underweight and was perfectly healthy. By the time she grew into a toddler and didn't care for milk anymore, I finally let go.

So, what happened with Lexi?

The second night was hell.

Her bassinet was beside our bed, and since I was breastfeeding, I was basically on call 24/7. But that second night? She didn't stop feeding. Every time I put her down – after winding her, of course, which I still hated with a passion – she would start crying. So I'd pick her up, comfort her, try to settle her. But she wouldn't settle. Feeding was the only thing that soothed her.

I think it's called cluster feeding.

Anyway, I was in bits. I was so exhausted from just giving birth – I hadn't slept in two days – and now my baby was using me as a human pacifier. Honestly, I think I could have killed Dan for sleeping so soundly next to me while I was nursing all night.

When I look back, I think that night might have been the trigger for what unfolded over the next few months. That fear crept back in – the fear that I'd never sleep again, that I'd have a baby who kept me awake every night, and that I'd lose all quality of life, unable to function from the sheer exhaustion of it all.

After that second night – thankfully – it didn't happen again. But I decided to do what I did with Mia: establish a good routine and sleep pattern. I really put in the work. Every evening at 6 p.m., I'd draw Lexi a bath, followed by a relaxing baby massage, then feed her and put her to bed around 7 p.m. That was the plan. Afterwards, I'd go downstairs to enjoy the evening with Dan. We'd cook, sit down with dinner in front of the TV, and watch whatever box set we were into at the time.

Sounds idyllic, right? Except I could barely get through a meal without running upstairs at the first cry. I'd pick Lexi up, settle her, and put her back down. I didn't feed her; I just comforted her. In those early days, I was running up and down the stairs at least ten times before she finally dropped off. But it worked. Dan took his turns, too. Over time, the trips upstairs became fewer until it was just one final 10 p.m. feed.

This is where it all went wrong for me mentally.

Lexi was an amazing baby – so good – but I created problems that weren't even there. I stopped breastfeeding after a few weeks because, like Mia, Lexi wouldn't unlatch. I felt like I was constantly feeding and had no idea how much she was getting. So, I switched to formula, which meant feeding her every three to four hours because, of course, that's what's *recommended.*

And just like with Mia, I needed her last bottle to be at 7 p.m., right before bedtime, to fit her *perfect* sleep schedule.

Writing this now, I can barely admit it to myself. I lost so many precious months because of what happened.

Lexi didn't seem to like feeding from the bottle – or so I assumed. When she did feed, she didn't drink much at all. That familiar sense of panic and déjà vu from five years ago came flooding back. I couldn't believe it was happening again. Feeding times became something I dreaded instead of moments to enjoy. I have no doubt Lexi picked up on my nervous energy every time I came near her with a bottle.

Whenever it was time to feed her, and I knew she was hungry, I had to lay her in my arms in front of the TV with *CBeebies* on to calm her down. Then, I'd slowly try to put the bottle in her mouth, hoping she'd latch on. Sometimes, it worked; other times, she'd just scream at the bottle.

I was a mess. Constantly crying, thinking there was something wrong with my baby. Yet, every week, I'd go to the health visitor, and sure enough, Lexi was gaining weight and perfectly healthy.

I tried switching formulas, just in case it was the taste or because one might upset her stomach. I was always on forums, scrambling for advice. Poor Dan didn't know what to do. He'd totally lost me.

I was obsessed. No one else could feed her but me. And on the rare occasions Dan tried, I'd hover over him, micromanaging every little thing. Some nights, when Lexi wouldn't finish her bedtime bottle, I'd sit on the bed and cry – sometimes even scream.

I'd built my own little hell.

Some nights, we'd put Lexi in her car seat, and Dan would drive around until she fell asleep. Then I'd feed her while she was half-asleep – just like I'd done with Mia. The relief I'd feel when she finished a bottle was addictive. And it only made the bad nights worse.

Most days were like this. Some were good, but the majority were bad.

Looking back, I know now – it was all in my head. Lexi was a good feeder, just like Mia had been. She simply didn't need as much as I wanted her to take. Sometimes, she'd guzzle the bottle down, and other times, she'd look at me as if to say, 'Get that thing out of my face right now.'

It wasn't about her sleep. Lexi slept through the night from 16 weeks old – the very first night we put her in her own room in her cot. And she's slept through every night since.

But still, my days were dark.

I was a shadow of my former self, filled with anxiety and dread. It was all I could talk about – to my mum, my sister, my friends – anyone who would listen. They tried to comfort me, but nothing could take away the constant pain in my throat or the weight I was losing from sheer anxiety.

Then the worst happened: the breaking point that I'm not even sure how I came back from. It was a Saturday, just two days before I was due back at *Hollyoaks* to resume my role as Cindy. I had 11 scripts piled up on the table that had been delivered to me, and I was dreading the day I had to return. With every envelope that dropped through the letterbox, the anxiety grew. I wasn't ready. I couldn't leave Lexi. I needed to take care of her.

Dan had agreed to take some time off work to look after Lexi so I could fulfil my contract with the show. He also thought it would be good for me – to get away, to step back into my old routine, to slip into being someone else for a day. Dan was the only person I trusted at that time to look after her and to do things the way I wanted them done.

That Saturday started like any other. Around lunchtime, it was time for Lexi's feed. The familiar feelings of anxiety began swirling in my stomach and tightening in my throat as I made up her bottle. I sat her on my lap in front of the TV, but something was wrong. Lexi wasn't interested. She screamed the house down every time I tried to put the teat in her mouth. So, I waited.

The hours dragged by, and we were well out of our routine at this point. I was a complete mess. Every time I tried to feed her, she just cried.

I was convinced something was wrong with her – *really* wrong. By the end of the day, eight hours had passed, and she still hadn't had anything. I had a complete mental breakdown.

Dan found me in the kitchen, screaming and smacking my head on the hard tile floor. I just couldn't take it anymore. I wanted it to stop. I believed, in that moment, that I'd be better off dead. In reality, I didn't want to harm myself, but I was so tightly wound with frustration and desperation that it all exploded out of me.

Dan called my mum. He didn't know what to do; he was desperate. When my mum arrived and saw me on the kitchen floor, she quickly called an ambulance. Dan tried his best to calm me down, but it was like a switch had been flipped.

The ambulance arrived, and my mum came with me to the hospital while Dan stayed to look after Lexi. Thank God Mia was with her dad that day. At just five years old, this isn't something I'd ever want her to witness or remember. I'm so grateful she didn't have to.

When we arrived at the hospital, I was taken straight to a bed in the emergency room, where I waited to be seen, and all I could do was repeat over and over again, 'Something is wrong with my baby. Something is wrong with her.' It never occurred to me that something might be wrong with *me*.

A doctor assessed me, and I told him everything that had been going on. He was very understanding and concluded that I had postnatal depression. He offered me a prescription for Prozac. At the time, I wasn't sure how Prozac was supposed to fix me. I tried it for a week, but it made me feel weird and even more anxious, so I stopped.

Looking back now, I know it wasn't postnatal depression that had hurled me to the depths of despair and triggered panic attacks. It was an anxiety disorder. It was the fear of future uncertainties based on imagined events. The presumption that something bad was going to happen – and my desperate attempts to control every situation so that the imagined bad event wouldn't happen. But in doing so, I manifested my own downfall.

I still have bouts of anxiety, but I've learned how to pull myself back before I go too far down the rabbit hole.

When I got home, Lexi had been fed and was asleep in bed – and this might sound strange considering what those four months had been like, but I can't remember it being any worse after that day.

My first day back at work was Monday, 10 January 2011. I remember walking into the makeup room and sitting in the chair. My hair had been cut and dyed into a short, sharp black bob with a full fringe. Cindy was back. Her 75-year-old millionaire husband had tragically fallen off a cliff while they were honeymooning in the Swiss Alps, making her a millionairess, potential murderer, and the Queen of Hollyoaks Village. I had some seriously high heels to fill.

Cindy was bigger and bolder than ever – the full-on rich bitch that everyone loved to hate. I had to dig deep, removing myself from my own personal circumstances to deliver the quick-witted, comedy-filled lines the writers had scripted for me. I was vulnerable. I felt small. I wasn't sure I could embody the opposite of what I was truly feeling.

After leaving makeup, I was walking toward the dressing room when I saw one of my co-stars, Ashley Taylor Dawson, who plays Darren. We'd known each other since we were teenagers, and when I rejoined the show back in 2008, our alter egos were entwined in a love affair with a Bonnie and Clyde kind of energy. We worked really closely together, and he knew me – the real me. He would call me out on my bullshit and help me see my potential.

When I saw him walking toward me, asking how I was and how Lexi was doing, I just looked at him without saying a word and broke down. I fell to the floor, having the most horrendous panic attack. He picked me up and held me, telling me over and over to breathe, that I was okay.

In between gasps and tears, I was spiralling, trying to pull myself together. I had a job to do. I'll never forget what he did for me that day. It wasn't anything specific; he was just there, and he cared.

After a lot of tears, I fixed my makeup, put on my costume, slipped my feet into Cindy's skyscraper six-inch black platform stilettos, and went to set. I nailed it. I had fun. I forgot, just for a few hours, the dark place my mind had been.

What I learned from that day is that mindset is an amazing thing. I shifted and embodied a woman who was full of confidence, sexy, successful, and completely unapologetic. Her comebacks were delicious. When I turned Cindy on, I felt that powerful.

I'm not saying that I went home to my family that night and was magically back to my old self, but every day that followed – every day I shifted my mindset to Cindy – I started to feel more and more empowered.

Things at home started to get a lot easier. Lexi was thriving and such a happy baby. As soon as the weaning process started, around five or six months old, my sister Rachel took over looking after her while I went to work, and Dan went back to his. That was a massive step for me – to let go and trust someone other than myself or Dan to take care of Lexi. But I trusted her.

My nephew Calvin, who's a couple of years older than Lexi, became joined at the hip with her. She absolutely loved it there.

As time went on and I got back into the swing of things at work, all the anxiety and negativity I had created slowly dissipated. My life shifted into a more positive place.

I truly believe I was meant to go back to *Hollyoaks* after just four months of maternity leave. I truly believe Cindy saved me. Without her, without embodying her and believing I was this confident, bold woman, I don't know what would've happened to me.

Maybe I would've eventually found a way out of my mental distress, but I believe I would've stayed stuck in a cycle of fear. Going back to *Hollyoaks* forced me to face my fears and step out of that loop. I had no choice but to show up and be Cindy, and because I committed and faced my fears, I broke out of my shell. I flew.

Sometimes, when you think you're falling apart, everything is actually working to help you fall into place. It's about moving out of your comfort zone, trusting, and embracing what's meant for you.

My children are my proudest achievement. They've both grown into incredible young women, even though they're worlds apart in who they are.

Mia is 19 now, navigating her way into the working world and learning to stand on her own two feet. She's embracing life and doing her thing – a fiercely independent girl with a strong work ethic. Right now, she doesn't know exactly what she wants to be, and that's ok. I know she'll figure it out. I sometimes catch myself offering her advice, thinking it'll serve her best, but I've come to realise that my dreams for her aren't her own. I have to let her figure it out in her own time. She still lives at home, but I know that, sometime soon, it'll be her time to leave the nest.

Lexi has just turned 14 and reminds me so much of myself at her age – before my mental health interruptions. She has a vibrant personality, always laughing. She's pushing boundaries, as most teenagers do, in such a rush to grow up, but she's always remained respectful and polite. She'd hate me for saying this, but she still calls me 'Mummy' and tells me she loves me every time she leaves the room.

Lexi, like me, loves the arts and is currently enjoying weekly acting classes. She has a natural talent for the stage and screen. And my God, she's beautiful – just like her big sister.

I love them both so much, and I feel so lucky to have a front-row seat to watch what difference they'll make in the world.

PART FIVE

Metamorphosis of Menopause

CHAPTER 13

The 4 a.m. Club

*I*t was the beginning of a new year, January 2021. I was in the throes of a new relationship with Tom, and I was the happiest I'd been in a long time. Love does that to you – everything just feels brighter, your face wears a smile like you've slept with a hanger in your mouth, and you exude a glow that everyone can see.

The first couple of times I shared a bed with Tom, I didn't sleep very well. Either he ended up sleeping in another room, or I did. I hated this. Being in a relationship, finally, with someone I could see myself sharing my life with, I never thought for a second that sharing a bed wouldn't be part of it. It felt so wrong, like a cruel twist in our love story. I also didn't expect a few sleepless nights to turn into two years of deprivation. It was like, one day, I had just forgotten how to fall asleep – like that part of my brain that enters another world for a few hours had turned off.

At first, it would take a couple of hours to nod off, but over time, that window between getting into bed and actually falling asleep got longer and longer. Eventually, I wasn't drifting off until 3 or 4 a.m. most nights. I say 'guessing' because I learned early on that clock-watching is like staring into the devil's soul – a self-inflicted torture of 'I have to be up in two hours,' knowing I'd spend the next day irritable, unfocused, and just plain miserable. It was horrendous, especially on workdays when I had an early call time on set. Two snatched hours of sleep? Not ideal.

I've had insomnia in the past, but it was always just a night here and there – nothing like what I was about to encounter.

When I had my kids, I thought they'd be the ones keeping me up all night, and they did for a while. But this? This was something else entirely, and I didn't see it coming.

For a month, I tried everything: hypnosis, sleep stories, natural supplements, over-the-counter medication – you name it, I tried it. Nothing worked. I even counted sheep! I dreaded bedtime, which probably made the problem worse. And because of my history, I know that the more you obsess over something, the bigger and more magnified it becomes.

Anyone who's dealt with insomnia knows the depths you'll go to. It becomes your primary focus – your obsession. For me, it was all I could talk about. And since I have no filter, I definitely lost my ability to read a room. I'd ask everyone about their sleep routines: 'What time do you go to bed?' 'Do you fall asleep straight away?' If someone told me they were a terrible sleeper too, I'd find comfort in the fact I wasn't alone while grilling them for their tips and tricks.

But then there were the people who'd say, 'I'm out like a light', or 'I'm gone as soon as my head hits the pillow.' Those comments? Oh, I could feel my hand clench into a fist as I imagined punching them in the face, their superior sleeping skills smugly lording over me. Tom is one of those people. And because I love him, I've had to work really hard not to resent him when he wakes up fresh and chipper after a solid seven hours of sleep.

What's even worse is when I haven't slept, and he's clearly had at least seven hours but still moans to me about his 'bad night' and how awful he feels. I've had to bite my tongue on more than one occasion. Honestly, though, I think I'm to blame for some of his restless nights. Yes, I became *that* girl – if I'm not sleeping, you're not sleeping.

When I'd been tossing and turning for hours, and Tom was fast asleep, I'd get so distressed from living in this 'awake-with-closed-eyes' cycle that I'd get out of bed and go wake him up, often crying and completely frazzled. 'Tom, Tom, I can't sleep, I don't know what to do,' I'd say while shaking him awake.

At first, I don't think he knew what to do. He'd pull me into his bed to comfort me, but then he'd very quickly fall straight back to sleep and start snoring – along with the dogs, Daisy and Lola. It was the marching band I absolutely didn't need, so I'd last about two minutes before heading back to my own little crypt of hell.

The solitude was unbearable. The world outside was sleeping, and there I was – wide awake, eyes closed, mind racing. I'd often open my eyes just to stare into the dark void of my eye mask, waiting for the miracle of sleep to finally arrive. Yes, I'm being dramatic, but stay with me here. Part of my brain would say, 'Just get up,' and the other part would shoot back, 'To do what?'

I hated reading – or, I should say, I'm a lazy reader. I love an audiobook; whoever came up with that idea is a genius. It used to take me forever to finish a book because I'm always on the go. My Audible library is packed with books that teach me something or help me grow personally. With everything I've been through with my mental health, taking care of it has become a priority – something I'll always work on.

But reading a book or listening to one wasn't exactly high on my list of things to do at 1 a.m., so I'd stay in bed, masked up, earplugs in, and just… wait.

By February, I'd only had a few sleepless nights here and there – I wasn't quite a fully paid-up member of the 4 a.m. club yet. But then my period was late. I've always been very on time in that department, so when a couple of days went by with no sign, I immediately did a pregnancy test.

All sorts of feelings rushed through me. I hadn't planned on having another child. It was a few days before my 43rd birthday, and the thought of being pregnant and doing it all again in my forties wasn't exactly on my list of midlife goals. My kids were at an age where they were becoming so independent – they didn't need me as much. I was almost through to the other side. I'd done the early motherhood bit, and my time to focus on myself felt so close.

The idea of hurtling back to day one on a 16-year-plus road of being someone else's whole world filled me with quiet anxiety. But here's the twist: when I peed on that stick, something in my gut *wanted* it to be positive.

Maybe it was because Tom didn't have children of his own – something he'd always said he didn't want. That was, of course, until he met me. When we talked about it, I couldn't help but smile at the thought of raising a family with him, maybe even bringing a son into the world.

Tom would be an amazing father. He's such a big kid himself, with a playful side my girls absolutely adore. And I know he'd protect them with his life.

When the test read negative, I was confused, to say the least. We hadn't exactly been careful, so I thought pregnancy could've been on the cards. A flicker of disappointment washed over me. I could tell Tom was disappointed, too.

I know we'd only been together for a couple of months, but we'd fallen in love so quickly. If it weren't for my biological clock ticking away, I'd like to think we could've had a serious discussion about it and maybe one day planned to have a baby.

A couple of weeks later, my period arrived. Maybe I'd just had my calendar wrong?

The insomnia continued. On rare occasions, I'd fall asleep within two hours, but most nights, I was surviving on just a few hours of broken sleep. On days when I wasn't filming first thing, I'd often catch up in the morning, which threw my body clock completely out of sync. I just wanted one day where I had the energy to do the things I loved – performing, working out, and stringing a sentence together over dinner with Tom. Insomnia was starting to rob me of my spark.

March rolled around, and once again, my period was late. And once again, I rushed to the pharmacy for a pregnancy test, baby names already swirling in my head. One toe dipped in fear, the other in, 'A year of maternity leave wouldn't be the worst thing.'

But this time, as I was taking the test, I started bleeding. I was more upset about being robbed of the anticipation – waiting for that positive line, imagining Tom's face light up with a mix of fear and excitement when I told him he was going to be a dad.

It was time to make a doctor's appointment and figure out what was going on. I didn't even mention the late periods – after all, that's all they were. I just wanted to sleep. I thought maybe I had a vitamin deficiency or low iron since I'm prone to anaemia. She suggested blood tests to rule out underlying causes and prescribed a short-term course of sleeping tablets to help re-establish a sleep routine.

This felt like a last resort. I didn't want to take anything I could potentially become dependent on. The tablets did help, especially on nights when I had to be up at 6 a.m. for filming. But going to bed at 10 p.m. to get a full eight hours was *hard*. I've always been a night owl.

I remember in my early twenties, living with my mum, staying up till 3 a.m. watching TV and then not getting out of bed until 1p.m. the next day. When I wasn't working on a show, my days were long and empty, so I'd fill the time bingeing. What a waste.

I could have used all that time to do something – anything – other than making myself sick. I could have started writing back then or learned a new skill. If I could go back to my younger self, I'd calmly tell her to get her head out of the toilet bowl and go live her best life (or, let's be honest, maybe not so calmly). It's so easy to say now, but at the moment? It's a mountain to climb.

I know that 20 years from now, I'll probably kill to be where I am today. I just hope that when I hit 66, I'm still sexy as fuck.

So, being a night owl, I thought, *Maybe this is just my natural sleep cycle. Could staying up late be the answer?*

Well, not if I wanted to keep my job. That said, I think insomnia should be recognised as a chronic condition. With a strongly worded doctor's note, surely 11 a.m. work starts should be a totally acceptable accommodation. 'Sorry, can't come in till 11 a.m. – I'm snoozing till 10.' If only.

Joking aside, I'd love nothing more than to be one of those people who go to bed at 10 p.m., wake up at 6 a.m., and have an energetic, productive day. But, honestly, with the number of times I get up to wee in the night, I probably hit my step count for the next day before sunrise.

I'm not trying to overshare about my toilet habits, but seriously – what *is* that? As soon as you hit 30, or have kids, your bladder turns into some kind of liquid dispenser. Every time I go, it's like my bladder's soaking up fluid from God knows where. And if I dare to drink two litres a day like I'm apparently supposed to because, you know, that's the magic hydration number, I might as well set up camp in the bathroom with a good book.

Over the coming months, I would learn so much about sleep. Let me tell you now, I'm one of those people who may as well have a degree in any subject interfering with my life because I will google the hell out of it – or, as it's officially called, *research* said complaint. And it doesn't stop there. Any supplement or new diet fad – keto, fasting, you name it – I was biohacking myself before it was on trend.

I was making bone broth in a slow cooker years before it became popular, and now you can't scroll through Instagram without someone promoting its health benefits. I'd like to add that I'm fully on board with this particular bandwagon because, honestly, I think bone broth is liquid gold, and it deserves its place in the spotlight. I also love the fact that my old friend Davinia is now a biohacking expert and has written two incredible bestsellers on the subject, which I devoured (aurally, of course). I have to say, I'm very proud to see her flying.

With all that said, I thought I was in perfect health. I started questioning some of the supplements I was taking but couldn't make a connection to insomnia. I stopped drinking caffeine – bye-bye, coffee. That was a tough one. However, I couldn't bring myself to give up red wine. I know, I know. Before all the sleep experts reading this think they've nailed the problem, yes, I know alcohol is a stimulant. It keeps your heart rate elevated and doesn't promote a good night's sleep. I'm fully aware.

But what am I supposed to do – cut *everything* out? Yes, probably. Am I not allowed to enjoy a couple of glasses of wine with my new love over dinner? Yes, probably. Stop having any kind of life? No. I enjoyed a glass of red over dinner, and it wasn't like it was every night. Sometimes, it helped me nod off; other times, I'd feel the dry mouth and dull headache before my head even hit the pillow. It really was a gamble. Wine wasn't causing my insomnia – it just wasn't helping.

I was told to call the Doctors surgery at least two weeks after my blood tests for the results. The receptionist put me through to the practice nurse, who went through them with me. From what she could see, everything was fine. All my levels were normal, although my iron was a bit on the low side – but nothing to be worried about.

'So, there's nothing wrong with me?' Not that I *wanted* an illness, but I needed some answers. I was so frustrated. I thought the answer to my sleep problems was on that bit of paper she had in her hands – that it would be something simple, something they could easily treat, and before I knew it, the world would make sense again.

Then she said something that confused me: 'I see that you haven't had your hormone levels checked?'

I had no idea what she was talking about. I'd avoided anything to do with hormones for most of my adult life because, as far as I knew, they just made you feel a bit crap once a month. Oh, and hormonal contraception made you fat, or so I thought, thanks to all the fearmongering I'd heard. That was pretty much the extent of my hormone education. Bravo, school curriculum.

The nurse suggested I get them checked because if I had a hormonal imbalance, this could be why I was having trouble sleeping. *Aha*, I thought. *That would make sense.* So, I booked in for another round of tests – another two weeks of waiting – and couldn't help shaking my head that it wasn't my doctor who'd suggested this in the first place. Could this be a simple fix? I mean, they're just hormones, right?

CHAPTER 14

What the Fuck Is Perimenopause?

It was results day. This time, I picked them up from the surgery. The receptionist handed me an envelope with my name and date of birth plastered across it. I got in my car, ripped it open, and scanned the information in front of me. Attached were my previous blood results, along with my hormone results. I had no idea what I was reading.

However, I did see the word *perimenopause* at the top of the second page.

'What the fuck is perimenopause?' I said to myself.

I knew what menopause was, but surely that was at least 20 years away. My whole life, I'd been told I looked so young – even now, people can't believe my age when I tell them. Looking young for 'my age' has always been something I thrived on. It made me feel good when someone would comment on it. So, how the hell am I here?

My mind couldn't comprehend it.

The most I knew about menopause was that you get to a certain age later in life, your periods stop, you get hot flushes, and then you move on to the next chapter. But I was still so young. I had more babies to make. Ok, maybe not that last part, but I'd have liked it to still be on the table as an option!

I was flustered about trying to make sense of what I was reading. None of it was computing. So, I went back into the surgery to ask if there was anyone who could explain my results to me.

What I learned that day was this: women go through perimenopause for up to 10 years before they hit menopause. During this time, we experience an array of symptoms that can pop up at any moment – including insomnia.

What?! So, was this the start of my 10-year journey of hell? Or was I halfway through and about to dive headfirst into midlife?

I was so confused. How is the word 'menopause' even in my vocabulary? I'm 43!

My head spinning, I left the doctor's surgery no closer to sleeping because, apparently, I wasn't a candidate for HRT. Why? Because I wasn't officially in menopause yet – just peri. Apparently, I'd have to go a whole year without a period before they'd even consider giving me any hormones to help balance my body.

Ok, great. So now I just have to wait it out? Wish my cycle away? Pray that each month, the most natural thing my body was born to do just decides to close up shop?

When I got home, I was in a state of shock.

How did I not know about this? Why has this never been a topic of conversation? None of my girlfriends knew about it, either. Why haven't we, as women, been educated on what happens in later life? I'm not speaking for all women here – maybe some of you reading this were brought up knowing everything that happens to you as a woman, from your first period to your last. But for me? All I ever learned in school was about the reproductive system. Even then, I didn't take in all the information.

No one told me a thing.

My mum had a hysterectomy at 40 and went straight into surgical menopause. I knew she had hot flushes, and I knew she was given HRT. But that's it. I didn't know anything else. It's almost like it's rude to ask – like menopause is this dirty little secret we're meant to go through in private.

From the research I've done since, perimenopause can start as early as your 30s – sometimes even younger – or as late as your 50s. I'd always assumed it was the latter. It seems odd, doesn't it? Half of the world's population will go through their own mini hell, yet we've not been armed with the information we need to prepare. It dawned on me that those late periods were not a sign of my womb preparing for another baby but rather for closure. That realisation shook me.

Since insomnia was my only obvious symptom, I began to wonder: *Could my bouts of anxiety over the past decade have been linked to my hormones?* Sometimes, anxiety would show up out of nowhere, even when my life was going great. I'd wake up with a tightness in my throat, struggling to catch my breath. Sound familiar? I tried everything – yoga, breathwork, meditation – but nothing seemed to work. Could all of this have been tied to a decline in my hormone production?

As the months went on and I was still nowhere near having a night where my bed felt like my best friend, I noticed a lot of talk in the media about menopause and how women going through perimenopause should be given HRT. Davina McCall, in my opinion, is a trailblazer for women in midlife. Her documentaries on the subject, highlighting our right to access hormones, have opened up a long-overdue conversation.

Now, feel free to geek out with me here, and if you're a man reading this, *please* don't skip this chapter. I truly believe men should be armed with this knowledge, too. Understanding that it's not 'her fault' but rather a case of crazy hormones on a rollercoaster ride could save a lot of relationships. It's not her choice to be on the 'Heatwave Express', but she's on board whether she likes it or not. And this train? It has as many as 45 stops.

Here's just a taste of what women might experience:

Decreasing Fertility, Anxiety, Brain Fog, Hot Flushes, Cold Flashes, Irritability, Depression, Insomnia, Bladder Weakness, Short-Term Memory Issues, Bloating, Body Odour, Poor Concentration, Itchy Skin, Vaginal Dryness, Breathing Issues, Burning Mouth Syndrome, Changes in Breast Size, Low Libido, Mood Swings, Panic Disorders, PMS, Reduced Motivation, Changes to Taste and Smell, Dental Problems, Dizziness, Dry Eyes, Dry Mouth, Fatigue, Headaches and Migraines, Heart Palpitations, Joint Pain, Reduced Bone Density, Muscle Tension, Nausea and Digestive Issues, Night Sweats, Recurrent UTIs, Thinning Hair, Tingling Skin, Tinnitus, Weight Gain, Acne, Pins and Needles, Changes to Skin Texture.

Wow! That's some serious shit we have to go through. Not every woman will experience all of it, but I'm sure there are a fair few on that list you could tick off.

By November 2021, my only symptoms were insomnia and anxiety. I hadn't yet done my usual deep dive into Google about perimenopause because I thought I had years before I'd need to worry about hot flushes and night sweats. But after eight months without proper sleep, I booked another doctor's appointment. This time, I saw a doctor who was very clued up on HRT.

I was dramatic – how could I not be? After eight months of barely sleeping and still having a regular period (which meant I wasn't technically in menopause yet), I was determined to get what my body needed. I thought oestrogen was the answer to it all. To my surprise, the doctor agreed and began discussing my options. Finally!

As she explained the gels, patches, and oral oestrogens, I settled on the gel. The idea of wearing a patch – and having to remember to change it every few days – didn't sit right with me. Plus, wearing something visible that would constantly remind me I was 'going through the change' wasn't appealing.

I was then told I'd have to take progesterone alongside the oestrogen because I still have a working womb. Now I was completely lost. All I learned in that doctor's office was that progesterone is needed to protect the lining of the womb from the build-up of oestrogen, and I'd have a bleed every month, just like having a regular period. She went on to say that some women don't tolerate progesterone well, but everyone is different. Then came the suggestion of the Mirena coil, which acts in the same way but without the monthly bleed, and it also works as birth control.

'So, if I have the Mirena, how will I know if I've gone through menopause if I'm not having periods?' I asked.

'You won't,' my doctor said.

Oh, well, that's useful, I thought. I mean, surely, I'd want to know if I was in menopause.

At that point, I had no idea about any of it, but I had to make a decision. Of course, I went for the Mirena coil with the added bonus of no periods and no babies. How was I to know I was about to have the devil implanted into my uterus?

Now, *that* is an uncomfortable experience. Mirena was implanted, along with the instructions: one pump of gel a day, increasing to two pumps in a month if necessary. That was it. That was all the knowledge I was armed with and I had no idea what was about to hit me.

I'm one of those people who needs a quick fix. Well, I *was*. I'd like to think I'm getting better at being patient. Okay, who am I kidding? I still need the quick fix. For instance, if I get a cold sore, as soon as I feel the tingle, even if I'm in the deepest sleep, I'll feel it. Then I'm scrambling around in the middle of the night for the Zovirax cream. A few hours later, that thing on my lip is still going nuts, growing at a rapid rate. I'll then google or YouTube, 'How to get rid of a cold sore fast?' You name it, I've tried it.

I'll stick anything on there, and if some 20-something YouTuber tells me it works, I'll sit all day with tomato ketchup on my lip, followed by ice, then apple cider vinegar, baking soda, and back to Zovirax, only to end up with a cold sore the size of my whole face. One time, I couldn't even film because it was so big. No amount of makeup or lighting could help minimise it. You get my point – instead of just leaving something alone to take its natural course and feeling uncomfortable for a short while, I stress, go into overdrive, and make everything ten times worse.

So, when it came to taking hormones, I expected to be Sleeping Beauty by night one. Of course, that didn't happen. I needed to be patient and let the miracle of HRT settle into my body. But I couldn't help wondering if this was what I'd been missing my whole adult life.

I've obviously screwed up my body from years of abuse: starving myself, binge-purge cycles, 25 years of all that stress. Surely, there had to be a consequence, one that I couldn't see. Any habit you create, good or bad, has an outcome eventually.

Within a month, I started to feel a shift in my body. It was uncomfortable. I could feel the anxiety building as each day went by. With the lack of quality sleep, I chalked it up to that – not the plastic device implanted in my womb pumping me full of synthetic hormones. That couldn't possibly be it, could it? I increased the oestrogen by another pump, as instructed by the doctor, if my symptoms didn't improve. Instead of improving, though, I felt like I was gaining symptoms.

We were coming to the end of 2021, ready for the Christmas break from filming, and the anxiety I was feeling had started to affect my mood. One day at work, I was chatting with Denise Welch, who was in the show at the time, about what I'd been going through. She suggested I speak with a hormone specialist and gave me a number. Denise handed me a lifeline, and I clung to it for dear life, hoping that this person could save me. A specialist was exactly what I needed.

We had a conversation where I explained everything that had been going on. She asked to see my blood tests, which I promptly sent via email. When she received them and looked over my levels, I'll never forget her response: '*Not peri-menopause.* **Very menopause!!**' The latter part was in bold as if to stress that I wasn't at the starting line but very much hurtling toward the finish.

This news devastated me.

She went on to say I needed to bump up my oestrogen to another pump because, being so young, I needed more. She also suggested some vitamins to help support my body and assured me I'd be fine. But I wasn't fine. I was a mess.

When Tom came over after work, he found me crying. I'd already told him what the specialist had said, and I think he was confused by my reaction. After all, I already knew I was in perimenopause, but I thought I had years ahead. This news confirmed my reproductive system was almost completely shutting down.

I didn't feel like a whole woman. I felt like I'd failed myself. I was only 43 – I was still so young. But this news most definitely slammed the door shut on ever carrying another child.

Tom did his best to comfort me, but he was in the dark as much as I was. He had no idea what I was dealing with, and he certainly had no idea his new fiancée was soon to become a shadow of her former self.

Happy New Year to me.

2022 had just kicked off.

People often use the new year as a time to reset the clock, implement resolutions, and commit to better habits while breaking the bad ones. Truthfully, you can do this at any time – any day, even now. But, true to form, I always put my eggs in the New Year basket. *'I will stick to my workout routines.' 'I will make better food choices.' 'I will watch my alcohol consumption.' 'I will show up for my loved ones.' 'I will listen.' 'I will meet Kylie Minogue and make her my best friend.'* You get the picture.

Then the first of January rolls around with a raging hangover, and the *'I'll do it tomorrow'* thought pattern kicks in. Motivation isn't the hard part – it's just doing it, even when it's hard. *Feel the fear and do it anyway.* That's my thinking now, but back then, my comfort zone and *'can't be arsed; someone else will do it for me'* attitude followed suit.

Every New Year, though, has always started with something to do with my weight, how I look, or *'This year, I'll find the cure for cellulite.'* It didn't matter that I was already slim and toned. Yes, I have cellulite, and yes, I hate it, but it doesn't define who I am. I always looked at my body like it wasn't good enough. I took it for granted.

And by the time I was deep into 2022, I would have given anything for my biggest concern to be just my cellulite.

CHAPTER 15

Love In the Line of Fire

Armed with my resolutions and good intentions, something wasn't feeling quite right. Looking back, it's hard to pinpoint exactly when the shift in my personality happened, and I don't remember being aware that I'd changed, but I had. Tom and I started arguing a lot more than usual. At first, I chalked it up to the usual relationship pitfalls everyone goes through. When you can no longer bring your best self to the table every day, irritations set in. It's inevitable that being around another person for long periods, they're going to get on your nerves. Now, I'm not saying I was an angel, but I couldn't see, at the time, my own demise in the reality I was living.

I had avoided hormones all my life, and by that, I mean contraceptive hormones. The synthetic ones that I always believed would make me blow up like a balloon. I'd heard so many stories from women blaming the pill for their weight gain that, for me, it was a big fat no. So now, having the Mirena implanted for reasons other than stopping me from reproducing and being told it was necessary to 'lawn mower' my womb (so to speak) from the build-up of oestrogen I was taking, of course, I was worried. I was convinced I'd blow up like a balloon.

This is where perspective comes in. When we face our mortality and our health is suffering, fearing a bit of weight gain is nothing. I'd take it in a heartbeat over what happened to me between 2022 and early 2023. I feel it's important to talk openly and honestly about my story because if any woman is suffering the way I did, I want to offer some light at the end of a very dark tunnel.

It's hard to know where to start. Reading this book so far, you'd think I'd have had enough mental health challenges to last a lifetime. But this time, I was facing something physical; something I didn't understand and something nobody, not even my doctors, seemed to have answers for.

Have you ever heard of the term 'the red mist'? That feeling when you're so angry it bubbles up from deep inside, rises to the top, and explodes like you've just blown someone's head off with your words. and all that's left in the air is the red mist. Well, that's how I felt if Tom so much as breathed in my direction. Ok, I'm exaggerating, but at the time, everything irked me, and Tom took all of my irritations personally.

What followed was a back-and-forth of non-communication, with no understanding of why the tiny thing we were arguing about escalated into something relationship-ending – on a week-to-week basis. Again, I'm exaggerating, but the phrase of 2022 was 'I'm done'. For me, when arguments reach the point of screaming at each other, my default is to end the relationship. I hate conflict.

One time, in a past relationship, I had an argument with a boyfriend that got so heated I said, 'I'm done,' got in my car, drove to the end of the street, stopped, and thought, *What the fuck am I doing? Where are you going? That's my house.* Driving back with my tail between my legs was not fun. I never wanted the relationship to be over; I just wanted the row to stop.

I couldn't tell you what any argument with Tom was about. I can't remember any details. It was never about anything big. Like I said, tiny niggles and irritations boiled up into something they never should have been.

One evening, we went out for dinner at our favourite restaurant. No negative words had been exchanged, but you know when you can just *feel* an argument brewing in the air? When the energy isn't quite right? After we'd finished eating – through very small talk – something was said that sparked something. A match had been lit. Then I set it on fire with a very firm, 'Fuck off, Tom,' and walked out, leaving him alone in the restaurant.

I got in the car, and everything in me wanted to drive off and leave him there, but I didn't. I waited. Tom eventually arrived, seeing me sulking in the passenger seat. He was not happy. So now what had been a fire turned into fireworks all the way home. I do believe I used the term 'I'm done' that night, followed by packing the few belongings I had at his flat. I stormed out and sat in my car, waiting for him to be the knight in shining armour, begging me not to leave. That was not the case. I waited and waited. Then I drove off, only to drive back again.

By then, I was furious – not just with him, but with the fact that he didn't chase after me or beg my forgiveness. I got out of my car and went back to his flat for round two. However, he had locked the door – and me out. Maybe throwing my key at him wasn't the best idea. I banged on the door. Nothing. I called his phone. Nothing. I sent a plethora of texts. Still nothing. So, with nothing left to do, I drove home, sobbing. Actually, *wailing* is a better word to describe the noise leaving my body. I didn't sleep at all that night. He had ignored me. He hadn't chased after me. The man went to bed and went straight to sleep. There's a high possibility he even fell asleep on the sofa while I was banging on his door.

Later, after we'd made up, Tom told me that if I had actually driven off and left him in the restaurant, he would have laughed and thought, *Fair play, I deserved that,* and respected me more for it. I'm yet to test that theory.

I'm very thankful Tom has never truly wanted to call it quits with me. He may have said it once or twice when we wound each other up to breaking point – like that night – but he never meant it. And neither did I.

Through the red mist and sleepless nights, I wondered, '*Is this it now?*' Still no closer to falling asleep within a couple of hours and rowing with my partner more than I'd like, how many years of this decline do I have to look forward to? What could possibly be next?

I thought the point of HRT was to ease, or even erase, the symptoms of menopause. But I felt like I was getting worse on the treatment. Only a year before, I'd been in the best shape and health I'd had in a long time. My energy was up. I felt in my prime. And now it felt like I'd skipped a few steps and dived straight into midlife without getting the memo.

I'd also started to gain weight. My stomach – which not that long ago had people asking how I got my six-pack – now looked like I was carrying a small watermelon. No matter how much I pulled it in, it popped out. I could've been mistaken for being pregnant. I started fasting, cutting carbs, and upping my exercise. I could feel myself breezing into dangerous, obsessive territory again.

I was so hard on myself. Not only was I arguing with Tom, but I was also constantly complaining about my weight and how unsexy I felt. That, in turn, had a knock-on effect on our sex life. Of course, I blamed the menopause. Yet, he understood and still told me I was – and still am – the sexiest woman he has ever met. I really didn't deserve him.

I feel like I took advantage of knowing how he felt about me. I pushed him, trying to make him see all the flaws I saw in myself just so I could be right, so I could prove he was being biased.

I think that if I had stayed in that frame of mind for too long, he would have seen my ugly. How can someone love a person who doesn't love themselves? It must have been so draining for Tom to keep picking me up. However, this was just the tip of the iceberg – things were about to reach a place I might not have come back from.

We were six months into 2022, and one night, while I was in bed doing my usual close-my-eyes-and-see-what-happens dance, I started to get this itching sensation that would jump around my body. I'd scratch one spot, like my leg, and then it would jump to my head, and so on. It was so annoying and lasted for hours until I finally fell asleep. At first, I didn't think much of it, but when it happened again the next night, I thought I had bed bugs.

I stripped the bed – which I absolutely hate doing. Honestly, when I was single, I would have had a relationship with a man just to have someone else tackle the duvet for me. Thankfully, Tom does it now. Anyway, after changing the bedding and washing myself down, it made no difference. The itching didn't stop. (I'm actually scratching myself now as I write this – it really is a mindfuck.)

The next morning, I drove to wherever sold bedbug spray and pretty much fogged my mattress when I got home. It was bad enough that insomnia kept me awake – I didn't need company. However, this was to no avail. Was I allergic to something? I remembered having this problem a few years ago, but only when I'd taken co-codamol painkillers. Something in the opioid caused itching in some people. Back then, it was just a one-off; it certainly didn't happen on consecutive nights.

I remember being at work, asking the production managers to please look at my schedule and, if possible, not have me in the first scene of the day just so I could get some rest.

They did help when they could, but when you're working on a television show, their priority is getting the scenes filmed. If I was needed on set for 8:30 a.m., then that's what I had to do.

One morning, I woke up after yet another night of itching and noticed that I was still feeling the spider-like crawling all over my body. I remember walking into Tom's living room, full of panic.

'Tom, I'm still itching,' I said, scratching my body like I had ants in my PJs.

I was full of panic – it's just my nature to go into full-on disaster, *the-world-is-ending-what-am-I-going-to-do* mode. Tom did his best to reassure me that I was okay, but how could he possibly understand how I was feeling or what it felt like? I'm sure he thought I was exaggerating or being overdramatic.

Deep down, I knew this feeling wasn't going to stop anytime soon. And I was right. What started as a few nights turned into days, weeks, and then months.

During this time, I had two rounds of blood tests done, and they all came back normal. Even my hormone levels were in a healthy range, thanks to the HRT. I was actually hoping something would show up – low iron, B12 deficiency, anything. I needed a name for what I was going through, something with an easy fix.

I felt so lost when the doctors couldn't help me. All they could do was give me a prescription for antihistamines, which were cheaper to buy over the counter anyway. Could it just be a symptom of perimenopause? I had read the extensive list of symptoms, and itchy skin was one of them. But surely I was given hormones to ease symptoms, right? And now, all of a sudden, I had this intense symptom out of nowhere.

I hadn't even had so much as a raised temperature, let alone a hot flash. What was going on?

As you can imagine, I spiralled into daily deep dives on Google, trying to figure out what the hell was happening to my body. I hadn't studied so hard since school. Honestly, I should have a PhD by now.

One day, while scrolling, I had a light bulb moment. It was the Mirena coil causing this. I had literally convinced myself that this was a fact. It was a foreign object placed inside my womb, pumping synthetic progestin into my body – of course, it had to be the Mirena.

I had joined a few menopause forums to find out if other women were going through the same thing and found that so many were experiencing severe side effects from the Mirena, including itching.

Faced with my self-diagnosis of 'itching by Mirena', I booked an appointment with my doctor – the same one who fitted it – for removal ASAP. But this left me with a dilemma. Once the coil was removed, I'd have to take progesterone for two weeks at the back end of each monthly cycle and have a period once a month. I had no idea how my body would react to progesterone, especially after reading countless stories from women on the forums about how progesterone intolerance was ruining their lives. They described feeling like shadows of their former selves. I was already slipping into that category, so I thought, *What the hell? I have nothing to lose at this point. Let's Russian roulette this thing and see which version of Steph I end up with.*

However, I did read that taking progesterone in the evening before bed helps aid sleep. Could this have been the answer to my sleep problems all along? Was I just missing some much-needed progesterone?

Maybe? I'll come back to this a little later.

Before having the coil removed, I made an appointment with the specialist I had seen earlier in the year to see if she could shed some light on my affliction. I took my recent blood tests to show her my hormone levels and told her what had been going on. I was still an insomniac and itching my way through day and night. She looked at my results and, although my oestrogen was quite high, she said that because I was so young and going through early menopause, my levels should actually be much higher. She explained that low oestrogen causes *formication* – the technical term for the feeling of spiders crawling over your body.

She said it *could* be the Mirena, but there was no definite answer, and it would ultimately be my decision whether to remove it. There are pros and cons to everything. She also prescribed a much higher dose of oestrogen in the hopes of calming my body down.

I left feeling hopeful; she was the expert, after all.

I started on the higher dose the next morning and kept my appointment with the doctor for the removal, which was a couple of weeks away. If the new dose worked and stopped the itching, I could keep the Mirena.

To my surprise, after a couple of days, I felt a bit better. I had more energy, and the skin-crawling sensation calmed a little. I even had a couple of good nights' sleep. I thought this was the turning point. All I needed was a higher dose. I clung to anything that could make it stop.

But just as soon as it went away, the crawling came back with a vengeance. It was as if the army of ants that had set up camp inside my body took a couple of days off to recruit reinforcements, returning with a whole new colony to wage war against me. Dramatic, I know, but I need you to grasp the severity of my predicament.

I was now adamant – the coil *had* to come out.

Appointment day arrived: 28 November 2022.

By this time, I had been itching for almost six months. I don't know how anyone put up with being around me. I would talk about it non-stop. I must have come across as so negative and moany. I cried often, especially at work. On set, I could feel the crawling beneath my costume. It was getting colder as winter approached, and I had to wear thermals outside. The itching was even harder to scratch when I was wrapped up so tightly.

What Tom went through when I couldn't sleep... hearing me cry so loudly from the other bedroom... He'd come in and beg me to stop. 'Please, just stop,' he'd say.

I'd scream at him that he didn't understand, and through snot and tears, I'd cry out, 'I just want it to stop. Please, make it stop.'

Sometimes, I'd go into his room to wake him up when I was distressed. I knew he couldn't do anything, but it was such a lonely, dark place to be. My thoughts swirled in my mind, and I needed a distraction. But more than anything, I needed sleep just so I wouldn't have to feel it anymore.

Explaining everything to my doctor, she was happy to remove the Mirena if there was even a slight possibility I was having a reaction to it. However, her biggest concern arose when she saw my stomach – it was so swollen that it raised alarms. She referred me to the hospital for an ultrasound to see what was going on.

Let me tell you, the removal of the coil is a lot quicker and less painful than the implantation. I was given progesterone to take in the evening since it would now be needed without the Mirena to shed the lining of the womb from the build-up of oestrogen. Feeling hopeful, off I went. Now it was just a waiting game. I prayed to God that this would finally be the answer.

Later that day, I went to the gym. While driving there, a rush of anxiety filled my body – it was awful. My throat felt so constricted I could barely breathe. What was going on now? I managed to push through my workout, but all I wanted to do was cry. I felt so sad. In all honesty, I was a complete mess, left wondering if I had done the right thing.

So, did removing the coil stop the itch-scratch cycle? The answer is a very sad *no*. In fact, things were about to get a whole lot worse.

Christmas was around the corner, and I couldn't believe how quickly the year had gone. Summer felt like yesterday, and I found myself yearning for the days when insomnia was my only problem. That's how serious my condition had become.

Just before Christmas, my skin started vibrating. The sensation was unbearable – like wild electricity running through my body. Tom had banned me from Googling symptoms, but I did it anyway when he wasn't around, like some dirty little secret. I needed to find a cure. I bought countless vitamins, tried a histamine-elimination diet, and did everything I could think of.

I couldn't even sit through an episode of anything Tom and I were watching without having to get up because I felt so uncomfortable. Relaxing was impossible. And bedtime? Bedtime was my darkest time. Nothing would switch off. My brain was on a relentless loop, and my body felt alive with this silent, buzzing energy that made me want to scream.

Christmas Day – usually one of my favourite days of the year – was a blur of trying to hold it together for my girls and Tom. I hadn't slept well, and the spider-crawling sensation was so intense. I was beating myself up, my vulnerability lay bare. I could see the frustration and helplessness in Tom's eyes. I know he would have done anything to take this away from me. He wasn't engaged to the person he had proposed to anymore, and I knew he wanted her back.

But he didn't give up on me – not once. Through the fiery arguments and the incessant crying, he was there, telling me how much he loved me and that I was everything to him. I wanted Christmas Day to be special, but all he could see looking back at him was my sad eyes.

We spent the day with my family, which was a nice distraction, but the quiet anxiety bubbled beneath the surface.

A couple of days later, things reached a breaking point – a day I will never forget. The doctor's surgery reopened, and first thing that morning,

I logged in online to book an appointment. I needed to see someone. I was desperate for help.

But there were no appointments available until the following day.

Tom was out with his friends for a day of Christmas celebrations. I didn't have my girls.

I was alone.

I drove to my house from Tom's flat, and I could feel something deep inside me building up, like a pressure cooker about to whistle. I entered my house, went upstairs to the bathroom, and then it happened – I had a full-on breakdown. I just wanted it to stop. I was screaming at the top of my lungs, 'Somebody, please help me! Please, please help me! Somebody make it stop!'

I wanted to die just to make it stop. I kept screaming, 'I don't want to be here anymore! Somebody, please help me!' The last time I cried like that was when I had been taken to the hospital over the anxiety I felt about Lexi and her feeding. This was a similar kind of grief, like someone had died. My reality at that moment was that I was doomed to feel this way forever, that it wouldn't stop, and my only way out was to not be here anymore.

I know I would never have harmed myself. I wasn't depressed; I just desperately wanted the crawling sensations and the vibrations to stop. In my desperation, I got in my car and drove straight to the doctor's surgery. I flew through the doors and begged for someone to see me. I must have given the receptionist quite a fright because of the state I was in. I was practically on my knees, begging for someone to save me.

I was taken into a side room while the receptionist went to see if someone was available. I calmed down slightly as the lovely woman who stayed with me spoke so kindly and sympathetically. Eventually, someone came, but not in the form I had hoped for. The doctor who was available specialised in mental health – which wasn't surprising since I had just announced to the entire waiting room that I didn't want to be there anymore.

As I sat opposite the mental health professional, it became painfully clear that she knew nothing about hormones, HRT, or menopause. How is that possible? As a doctor, regardless of your speciality, you should at least know the basics of what happens to every second person in the world when they reach the halfway mark in life. Instead, I was grilled about my mental state.

Through tears, I tried to explain that something was happening in my body that no one could fix, and I just wanted it to stop. I couldn't live like this anymore. Okay, maybe it was fair to have 'The Priory Mental Health Hospital' on speed dial at this point, but for me, it was simple. If the itching would stop and I could finally get more than four hours of sleep, I would be the happiest person in the world. I wasn't depressed. I didn't need antidepressants – which, of course, were offered. I needed someone to tell me it was going to be okay. I needed someone who understood what was happening to me and knew exactly how to fix it.

I left the surgery slightly calmer than when I'd arrived, but I was still a mess. My overriding thoughts were so intrusive, and there was nothing I could do to stop them. It sounds so easy when people say, 'Just think positive thoughts, and you'll feel better.' The idea is that your reality shifts to something happier if your mindset does. I believe there's truth to that, which I'll talk about later, but at that moment in my life, it felt near impossible even to raise a smile, never mind think positively.

February rolled around, which is my birthday month – five days after Valentine's Day, the 19th. Tom loves celebrating birthdays more than Christmas, which he isn't really a fan of, while I am the complete opposite. I love Christmas, but birthdays? Not so much now that I'm hurtling rapidly towards 50. That said, I do love being spoiled. I'm very much a gift giver, but it's nice when someone knows you well enough to gift you something meaningful. Tom is very good at this and has always blown me away with his thoughtfulness.

This particular birthday in February 2023 landed on a Sunday. He had the day and night planned to a T. I was told we'd be staying somewhere overnight and had two amazing meals lined up. The first was lunch at Hawksmoor in the heart of Manchester, famous for its steak, and the second was a few hours later at a restaurant called Six by Nico, known for its tasting menu paired with wine for each dish. We'd be staying at the Dakota Hotel, which had been high on my list of places to stay.

It all sounds so amazing, doesn't it? I wish I could tell you I had the most wonderful day, that I soaked up every minute with Tom but I didn't. In fact, I barely made it through lunch. When we arrived, we had to wait for our table, so we sat near the bar with a glass of wine. All I remember is crying. I sat there, on my birthday, in this beautiful restaurant, and cried. Tom did his best not to get frustrated with me. He had been looking forward to this whole day, but his fiancée was ruining it.

Why couldn't I have just sucked it up for one day? The itching wasn't leaving my body anytime soon, so why not go with the flow and enjoy the food, the wine, the company? During lunch, he asked me if I wanted to go on with the rest of the day. I said no, and he took me home.

I feel so sad writing this. It's so easy not to enjoy life, to wallow in self-pity, to be selfish, and not see what's going on around you. I can't redo this. I can't take it back. There are no do-overs – just lessons.

When I was working, I always considered myself professional. Yes, occasionally, those lines would blur. In the world of television, especially in soap, we're considered one big family. Everyone looks out for each other – cast and crew. If you have a problem, someone is there to lend an ear or wipe away a tear. But over the last nine months at that time, I must have driven people crazy with my constant bitching and moaning about my hormones and the menopause, like I was the only one going through it. I was constantly searching for answers from others.

I never broke character while filming, though. I showed up, and I was Cindy, despite wanting to rip my body to shreds. I'd find myself watching everyone on set, looking to see if anyone else was scratching an itch, just so I could normalise it somehow – like, it isn't just me. For nine months, I showed up.

Until one day in March 2023.

I had a full day of scenes. It was early morning, and I was shooting in the village. I was quiet. The director was talking through the scene with me and the other actors. I could feel something bubbling inside me. My body was tingling and vibrating underneath my thermals and thick red coat. As I walked through the scene, I could feel the tears beginning to well up. I remember thinking, *Don't do it. Not now.* But I was powerless to stop it.

The director, Sean, and the first assistant director, Colin, saw immediately that I was not okay and quickly ushered me off the set. I had a complete meltdown, similar to the one I'd had at the doctor's just after Christmas. I kept saying over and over, 'I don't want to be here anymore. I just want it to stop.'

Neither Sean nor Colin knew what I was going through personally – not to this extent, anyway. But I think, across the board, people on the show were aware that I was not okay.

A production manager was called down to see me. She told me I could go home if I didn't feel like carrying on, but what was the point? It wouldn't stop at home – I wouldn't have anything there to distract me. I told her I'd carry on and get my scenes done.

However, in the afternoon, I was on a different shoot. There was a freelance assistant director on this one called Jo, and that afternoon, she saved me. While I had managed to pull myself together earlier, all the emotion was still running through me. Halfway through shooting the scene, I broke down, tears cascading down my face. Jo immediately called, 'Cut,' and took me off that set and into another one next door. She thought I had depression, but as I told her my story and explained what had been going on, she said, 'I know someone who can help you. My sister had exactly the same thing, and this man saved her.'

His name is Dr. Michael Barnish. She quickly called her sister and got his personal number. That afternoon, I was on the phone with someone who said, 'Don't worry, I can help you.' Those were the words I had been longing to hear for the last nine months.

What I learned that afternoon was music to my ears. He diagnosed me with oestrogen dominance. He explained that I had a soup of oestrogen swirling around my body and not enough progesterone to balance it out and clear the excess. This made so much sense to me. I immediately felt calmer as I booked an appointment with him for what I jokingly called a 'full-on oestrogen exorcism.'

I was told to stop my hormones immediately so my body could return to baseline, and we could go from there. He also instructed me to take two antihistamines every morning with vitamin C and psyllium husk – I needed the fibre to help eliminate any excess histamine. I wasn't allowed to eat or drink any high-histamine foods, either.

What he explained to me was the ultimate lightbulb moment – and coming from a man, it was even more surprising. Since learning about menopause and hormones, all the focus had been on oestrogen, as though it was the saviour of all things. But he told me that progesterone is the first hormone to start declining in perimenopause. This was my lightbulb moment.

Progesterone is responsible for calming us, relieving anxiety and depression, helping us sleep, supporting bone health, and improving skin! It increases oil production, slows the ageing process, and can even help with weight gain, migraines, joint pain, and PMS. The list goes on. No wonder, for the ten years before the real chaos hits, we think it's something else. Anxiety? Depression? We're offered antidepressants. Weight gain creeping in even when we're living on lettuce and being gym machines? Insomnia?

We're losing our progesterone while pumping ourselves full of oestrogen, throwing everything completely out of balance. That imbalance causes so many symptoms, not the menopause itself.

There are so many women out there who believe they're progesterone-intolerant. Maybe some are, but our bodies have naturally produced progesterone since puberty during the second half of our cycle, the luteal phase. Were these women intolerant of their own bodies before the decline started?

I don't claim to be an expert – not even close. But this just made sense to me. I fully understand that synthetic forms of progesterone, known as progestins, can cause intolerance. The Mirena coil caused so many unpleasant symptoms for me.

Did you know that when you take progestin, it halts your body's natural production of progesterone? Crazy, isn't it?

So the plan was for me to get back to baseline and then start introducing progesterone only on days 14 to 28 of my cycle, when the luteal phase was due to start, to help get my natural cycle back on track. Navigating this wasn't so easy. I hadn't had a natural period for a year with the Mirena coil, and they'd become so irregular I had to start using the moon cycle. Thankfully, the itching stopped. I can't pinpoint when I just stopped feeling it or thinking about it, but it was gone. I also started to sleep. I can't tell you what a relief it was to finally get my life back. Falling asleep without fear or panic was the best gift I could ever receive.

They say in life, things happen for a reason. Sometimes you make a wrong turn, the wrong decision, and you have to navigate your way through the shit to see the flicker of light at the end of the tunnel. It sets you back on the path that's your purpose, the path you were meant to be on. They say in the hardest times is where growth happens. I do believe this to be true – it builds strength for future hardships. I don't know what my lesson was to learn from this. Maybe it was to teach me something, to arm me with all the knowledge I needed to avoid making another wrong decision.

Hormones are a minefield, and every one of us wonderful women is made up completely differently. We need hormones tailored for us, not given a one-size-fits-all approach. When I started to introduce oestrogen back into my body, I was so nervous, but I knew that with caution and the lowest dose, I'd find what worked for me. I started on the lowest dose on Day 1 of my cycle (or the moon cycle), just for two weeks, and then continued with progesterone for the latter two weeks of my cycle, mimicking what my body would naturally do.

It was very clear to me after a few weeks that my body didn't need a huge amount of oestrogen at all. Everything started to fall back into place. I had a lot more energy, I lost some of the weight I had gained, my temperament was a lot calmer, and I felt like me again. What I didn't know was that a mere five months later, I was to have my last period.

I remember the day so well. It's a strange thing to remember. I don't remember the last time I played outside with my friends as a child. I don't remember my last sleepover. I don't remember the day I packed up my Barbie dolls. I don't remember the last time I called my mum, 'Mummy.' But somehow, I remember the last day of my period.

Maybe it's because I was filming a scene in the hospital set where Cindy was being treated for a manic bipolar episode. (If any *Hollyoaks* fans are reading this, it was when Cindy was hallucinating that Luke was still alive and was with her in the hospital.) I remember wearing a silk dressing gown. It was green and cream with purple flowers on it. Nick Pickard, who plays Tony, said to me, 'What's that on your dressing gown? Haven't shit yourself, have you?' He was laughing, and I took it the way it was meant – a joke. He wasn't being serious. That's just his nature; he's one of the funniest men I know.

But at that moment, when I looked behind me and down at my dressing gown, I knew exactly what it was: blood. I had leaked through my costume. I quickly gathered myself and retorted, 'No, it's blood. I'm on my period.' I was embarrassed. I ran to the toilets to sort myself out and gave my dressing gown to one of the girls in the costume department to clean it. I felt so bad.

Nick had no idea, and he must have felt embarrassed himself. He's since told me he was mortified. I had never leaked before – not to the extent that it was visible for anyone else to see. That particular period was so heavy. I was grateful for it, though. I felt like I was still in my prime, that my womb hadn't packed up on me just yet.

But as I waited the following month, and then the one after that, and the one after that, it became clear to me: I had, in fact, gone through menopause.

My last period was August 2023, and as I sit here writing this at my kitchen table in November 2024, I can say that although I had a few mild hot and cold flashes for a couple of months after my cycle ended, they didn't last. I was told to introduce progesterone full-time in the evening and to continue on the small dose of oestrogen. I did just that, and the flashes stopped.

Since then, I've felt more balance in my body than I have in years. I am truly grateful for where I am right now and how I feel in my body. I weathered a storm to get here, but I'm here, knowing my body and myself better than I ever have before.

If you are a woman reading this and you see yourself in any part of my story, I hope I've given you some clarity. While we may not be the same, and what works for me may not work for you, the advice I would give you is – go slow. Don't be in a rush to find the answer. Listen to your body and its needs. Our bodies are so wise – they have a way of telling us when something is wrong. We just have to listen.

I've been guilty of not listening. Maybe you have, too.

As for Tom and me, we survived the line of fire. This man loved me when I didn't even know myself, and for that, I'll be forever thankful. He always knew I was still in there, even in the midst of the minefield.

PART SIX

A Life Rewritten

CHAPTER 16

Flipping the Script

$\mathcal{I}$ wrote the introduction you read at the beginning of this book within a week of receiving the news that Cindy was being axed from *Hollyoaks*. That was nine months ago. As I sit here now, approaching December 2024, I could never have imagined a more different life than the one I've been living for the past 16 years.

When I wrote down the events that happened in that room, I never intended to write a book. It just happened. Every day, I would show up to my computer and write. It was so therapeutic to get it all out onto the page. At first, I was writing about finding my happiness – chasing something and never being fulfilled. The chase that keeps you in a constant cycle of never being satisfied:

'I'll be happy when I'm skinny.'

'I'll be happy when I'm famous.'

'I'll be happy when I find love.'

'I'll be happy when I'm a mother.'

'I'll be happy when I'm through menopause.'

'I'll be happy when I'm axed?'

There's a question mark on that last one because I had no idea I would find my *happy* when I lost the one thing I thought was my life.

Each part of this book is about those very titles, but as I wrote, I realised that finding happiness isn't about reaching the goal. It's about the journey to get there, about finding happiness in the moment.

Trust me, this is not easy. It may sound simple, but it's not. Like anything in life, you have to figure it out step by step. So, when I found out my fate on that day in March, I flipped the script. I knew my life was about to change in a matter of a few short months, and I was the only person in control of what my new future would look like.

What was I going to do?

I started writing. Every day, I showed up at my computer and wrote my story: my movie, my ups, and how I picked myself up from my downs. I've had mental illness plague my life. I've held myself back because I didn't believe I was good enough. But writing about myself, looking back on each piece, has helped me see it all as part of the puzzle I've been putting back together to make it fit.

Now I understand: it's only me telling myself I'm not good enough. It's up to me to show up for myself and tell myself I am. I accept full responsibility for my life and the choices I've made – even the choice to believe other people's negative opinions. That has always been my choice.

This was a huge wake-up call.

I've spent so many years looking for someone or something else to blame – whether it was another person or the circumstances I found myself in.

When I was axed, I had a choice: sink or swim. I chose to swim.

I took a week off after finding out my fate. I didn't want to go back in on the Monday without figuring out my feelings about it, only to have everyone tell me how sorry they were. My gut was telling me this was the right thing. I didn't know it then, but I had been unhappy for a very long time.

Of course, I loved my job. I loved performing. I loved having the security and a regular paycheck. But after 16 years, I didn't feel challenged anymore. There was no growth. I wanted to feel free again, to try something new – whether that was another role or something completely different.

I didn't want to grow old on the *Hollyoaks* set without exploring anything else. I had bigger aspirations. and writing about my life and what I had achieved has solidified what my future potential could be, I just didn't know it until I was told my services were no longer needed.

Sometimes in life, you need to be pushed rather than jump.

I was always so scared to leave. I felt that if I chose to, I'd be letting down everyone who loved Cindy. I couldn't bring myself to hang up her heels. I also had no idea what to do with my life, of course being an actress is in my blood, and I will never leave the career I have built behind, but I know there is more out there to learn and experience. However, the feeling of not knowing what was next terrified me more than anything – stepping outside my comfort zone.

I felt safe in my *Hollyoaks* bubble. But since leaving, I'm not sure there was any safety in staying.

In the week I took off work to come to terms with my fate, I started to write. I knew there had to be a reason for this book. I didn't want to write a self-indulgent novel about my life and what had happened to me – I wanted to finally learn about myself, to understand who this ever-changing self is. I also wanted to inspire anyone who identifies with any of the struggles I've had.

I truly believe that if you desire something enough, the universe will find a way to give it to you. I had a strong desire to help myself and, in turn, help others.

During that week, I don't know why, but something compelled me to type 'life coaching' into Google. The Jay Shetty Certification School popped up. Intrigued, I watched one of the videos about how becoming a life coach can not only change your own life but also the lives of others. Jay talked about his mission to change a billion lives, and it had me at 'hello,' and something inside me knew that I wanted to be part of that mission.

But I didn't dive in just yet. I know I have a tendency to *do* before I *think* sometimes, but I still had three months of filming left to do at *Hollyoaks*, and committing to studying wasn't something I was sure I could fit into my schedule – especially since I'd also made a commitment to myself to write this book, a promise I didn't want to break.

Instead, I signed up for the email videos. Every day, a new one of Jay Shetty's words of wisdom would drop into my inbox, enticing me to make a change.

I believe in signs from the universe and seeing them when they show up. You can either take action or let the opportunities pass you by. I've done both throughout my life. When I've desired something so much that it becomes my primary focus, I've recognised the signs and taken action. But there have been times when something appeared, and I ignored it – usually because of the state I was in at that moment.

At this point in my life, knowing that in just 12 weeks, I'd be unemployed for the first time in 16 years, I was very open to receiving and taking action. So, one day in early April, after watching another inspiring video from Jay, I clicked on the 'enrolment interview' box just to see what it was all about.

My call lasted around 40 minutes, and by the end of it, I knew this was what I wanted to do – not as a replacement for my acting career but as something meaningful I could pursue alongside it.

As soon as I was enrolled, I had immediate access to the coursework. The course was broken down into 11 modules, with an exam at the end of each one. I needed to complete all 11 modules, at least 33 hours of self-study (including webinars with mentors discussing various topics), a minimum of 20 hours of unsupervised coaching, and attend eight mandatory cohorts with my designated mentor – all before the final exam. This all had to be completed within four months.

I hadn't studied for anything in 30 years. 'Overwhelmed' is an understatement. I felt sick at the thought of coaching someone so soon. I feared I wouldn't know enough to hold an hour-long session, let alone one that was being recorded.

But I immersed myself in the process. Just like anything in life, you don't know what you're doing at the start. But bit by bit, step by step, every day, you take in the knowledge. This habit of showing up eventually becomes mastery. It's like learning to drive. When you first got behind the wheel, did you know what you were doing? For most of us, the answer is no (unless you're Tom, who was self-taught and thinks he is a Jedi). But after showing up and learning, driving is now effortless (well, for some of us, anyway).

I became my first client before I started diving into anyone else's world. I needed to figure out my own mess of entangled beliefs, learned behaviours and who I fundamentally was now.

I took my laptop to work every day, studied in between scenes and at lunchtime, and immersed myself in the course whenever I had spare time.

Every lesson I dug into required me to go deep within myself. It wasn't easy – there was so much I had to take responsibility for. In fact, all of it. No one made me stop eating at the age of 13. Yes, there was an underlying reason, but it was still my choice to eat less. No one forced me to binge incessantly or spend most of my adult life with my head in a toilet bowl. No one forced me to take to heart every negative thing ever said to me. Every single choice I made was mine.

This revelation blew my mind. For so long, there was always something or someone to blame for the wrongs in my life. And I think a lot of people feel this way, too. 'It's not my fault' has probably left my mouth more times than the food I was throwing up.

However, please don't misinterpret what I'm saying. I fully understand that sometimes, our choices are taken away by the actions of others. When it comes to any form of violence, I've been fortunate never to have experienced anything so horrific, so I can't speak to how I would feel or how someone else should cope. I can only speak to my own personal trauma and what I invited into my life – and didn't ask to leave.

When it came time to coach for my unsupervised hours, I could source my own clients – referrals from friends or anyone willing to try free coaching. It was also common practice to coach within the school with other students, which gave me the opportunity to meet some incredible people from all over the world. These were individuals I never would have crossed paths with if not for this community of like-minded people. I've taken away some beautiful friendships and, to this day, I still jump on Zoom calls with a few of them for coaching or just catching up.

Amanda from Texas – an amazing lady – was the first woman to coach me, and I'm so thankful to her for letting me flow. In turn, I got to coach her. Then there's Natalie from the UK. What can I say about Nat? I remember posting in the school forum, asking if anyone in the UK wanted to coach each other. Being in the same time zone made scheduling so much easier. Natalie answered my post, saying she'd just started her unsupervised sessions and would love to coach me. She left her email, I got in touch, and that began a beautiful relationship.

We couldn't be more different, yet we're so alike. Our industries and lifestyles are worlds apart, but coaching became the foundation for something extraordinary. Natalie has become one of my closest friends. We haven't met in person yet, but we schedule regular catch-up calls – more often than not, just to chat rather than coach.

When you coach someone, you leave all judgement at the door. You're completely unbiased. You're there to listen and guide in whatever way your unique style allows. Through the process of coaching, Natalie and I got to know each other very quickly. We'd always stay on the call long after the session was over, saying all the things we couldn't during the recording. We even took our final exam at the same time so we could get our results together.

I remember that day so clearly. I was so nervous. Natalie had done hers just before me and told me not to worry, that I had this. Everything came down to that one final exam: all the hard work, all the effort. Tom was out with friends, so I had the house to myself. I took a deep breath, told myself I could do this, and sat down at my computer, shaking like a leaf the whole way through.

It had been years since I'd taken an exam, and I never thought of myself as particularly academic. That awful imposter syndrome started creeping in. What if I failed?

After I finished, I thought it would take up to 24 hours to get the results. I couldn't sit in the house waiting, so I went out to meet Tom for a drink to take the edge off. After I arrived and had chilled out a bit, I checked my email – and to my surprise, my results were already in.

I had passed. Not just passed – I scored a stellar 92%!

I was so elated I couldn't breathe. I was so proud of myself for doing this. At that moment, I felt like I could do anything.

Natalie passed, too, with the same high result as me. I am so grateful to have met this incredible woman, and I hope she will always be in my life. Another special lady from the coaching world is Bryce from Colorado. We met through our cohort groups. She messaged me privately after one of our sessions, saying she wanted to reach out because she resonated with everything I brought to the calls. She told me she enjoys my perspective and loves hearing what I have to add, and she wanted to chat more.

This led to us coaching each other. Bryce is my spiritual friend, someone who is on her own path of self-discovery. She helps me tap into my spiritual side so effortlessly. Every session with her leaves me feeling lighter, with my mind, body, and spirit aligned.

There are so many other people I've met along the way, and to all of you – thank you for being a part of something so transformational, not just for me but for all of us.

Every day that I was working, I had the biggest smile on my face. I didn't fear leaving. In fact, I was excited by it. I was learning not only a new skill but also unpacking all of my own trauma, eating disorders, and limiting beliefs. It has been life-changing. Like I said, I was my first client. I've done all the work on myself – and I'm still doing it.

So many of my colleagues would ask if I was okay. Their words would wash over me, and I could feel their pity. 'Never been better,' I would often reply. Or I'd tell them I was excited to leave, that it was the right thing for me. And I one hundred per cent believed that to be true.

I was wrapping up my old life while being excited about starting a new one – whatever that looked like. I took it one small step at a time, and I believed in myself. I could do it. Not once did I break down or pity myself.

It wasn't just me losing my job, and I never lost sight of that. I hoped that those who were also leaving would feel my positivity, flip their own scripts, and believe that there is, in fact, life after *Hollyoaks*.

CHAPTER 17

Will You Marry Me – Twice?

When I was given my exit storyline, I already knew how Cindy would leave the show – exactly how she left the first time, fleeing to Spain, where she'd found a home back in 2000 to 2008, this time taking her little brother Tom with her. I didn't expect a big, explosive exit. Had I chosen to leave on my own terms, and if they weren't wrapping up a year's worth of storylines with other characters ahead of the time jump to the future, I absolutely would have loved an iconic exit. Why not? Cindy is an icon. I wanted to see her burn the village to the ground, leaving a trail of devastation in her wake.

But with everything that had happened, I just wanted to leave and get on with my life. Something was waiting for me, and I couldn't wait to discover it.

My leaving date was set for 3 July. I had my final scripts and the end in sight. Tom and I had been talking about going on holiday, so as soon as I knew my leaving date, we started looking for the perfect getaway. I couldn't wait to escape and have some downtime with him. I reached out to the travel company Blue Bay because Tom had been getting so many emails from them with great deals – many in the Caribbean and the Maldives.

The Maldives had been on my bucket list for years, though I'd always imagined going there on my honeymoon. I got in touch with Blue Bay to see if they'd be interested in a collaboration, and to my surprise, they said yes! I was so excited about the opportunity to work with them and visit places I'd only dreamt of.

As Tom and I sat down to go through the listings they sent us – most of them in the Maldives – we landed on one particular place called Ifuru Island. It was relatively new, and everything about it just felt right, so we promptly booked it for a week after I was due to leave the show.

As part of the package, they offered an upgrade and a free wedding – something neither Tom nor I ignored. Not long after booking, I was driving to the gym when Tom called me from work. As I pulled into the car park and answered his FaceTime, he asked, 'What do you think about getting married?'

I didn't hesitate. I said yes.

Oh my God, we're getting married! I felt so excited. We didn't tell anybody what we were planning apart from my children and our parents. We knew getting married in the Maldives wouldn't be legally binding, so we planned another wedding at home so that our family and friends could celebrate with us.

That wedding would be held at our favourite restaurant, The Coast, in Prestbury – somewhere we'd previously discussed as the perfect wedding venue. I felt like both of my wedding dreams were about to come true, and they did.

At the same time, my house was in full renovation mode. The side extension had been completed, and it was almost time for all the interiors to be ripped out and refurbished. I'd been living in a mess for the last eight months and couldn't wait for it to be finished. More importantly, I couldn't wait for the bills to stop.

Lisa, my interior designer, told me that while we were away for two weeks, the majority of the work would be completed. She assured me that when we returned, we'd come back to a brand-new home.

This was music to my ears. Not only were we getting married, but Tom would finally be moving in with me as my husband. It felt like everything was falling into place so effortlessly – and it really was.

There was no stress. I found a wedding dress with the help of my designer friend Carrie from Rene Couture. I've never really pictured what my wedding dress would look like. I didn't have a specific style in mind. I sent Carrie pictures of different dresses with similar themes I liked, and she suggested I get in touch with Jazmin from Flamingo Bridal in Liverpool.

When Jazmin and I connected, I sent her the same pictures. Almost immediately, she found me *the* dress. The beauty of it was that even though it looked heavy, it was as light as a feather – perfect for a wedding day in the sun.

Wrapping up *Hollyoaks*, studying to become a life coach, renovating a house, and planning *two* weddings, you'd think I'd have been pulling my hair out, that I'd spread myself too thin. But honestly? I had never felt so alive.

The time was fast approaching for me to say goodbye to my old life. The day was Wednesday, 3 July 2024. When the last 'action' was called, followed by the final 'cut', and I heard the words, 'And that's a wrap on Stephanie Waring,' it felt like an out-of-body experience – almost like it wasn't happening.

A slew of people filled the room to say goodbye. Hannah, the executive producer and the one who'd delivered the news of my exit, handed me a bottle of champagne and a bunch of flowers, followed by a speech. Sixteen years summed up in a few sentences. That's the truth of it. But it was lovely to hear how far I'd come with Cindy, a legacy I am so proud of.

I cried as I left the building, knowing I wouldn't be returning. But the tears left me as quickly as they came, replaced by a euphoric sense of freedom and excitement. What now? Even though I was training to be a life coach, at that moment, I felt like I could do anything. I could sleep in a little longer, drink on a school night, cut my hair – oh, I couldn't wait to try a new look without having to ask permission!

If I hadn't taken action and dreamt of something better for myself, I think I would've held on a little tighter and mourned a little longer. I'm so grateful I didn't give up on myself. I'm yet to truly mourn, yet to shed a tear. There are days when I do feel lonely; I'm so used to being part of something that required me to be social, interacting with people daily. Now it's just me, working for me. But I love the quiet. I love working on the parts of myself I couldn't see before – the blind spots that are now so visible.

With Cindy in my rearview, Tom and I began our journey to the most special place we've ever been in our lives: Ifuru Island, Maldives.

We had been liaising with Rochelle, the project manager on the island and the woman responsible for creating the magic of the resort, and Sinnu, who was working with me on the PR for the trip and organising everything wedding-related. Tom and I were in very good hands – we didn't want for anything.

Everything about this trip was magical. From the moment we arrived, when Sinnu picked us up in a Barbie buggy and drove us to our own piece of paradise for the next two weeks, it was perfect. When we arrived at our front door – room 406 – I was literally stunned by my surroundings.

In the middle of one large room was a huge king-size bed with the words *Welcome to Ifuru Island* spelt out in flowers. The bed faced a verandah with its own private pool. Behind the bed were the wardrobes and dressing area, with a door that opened into an outdoor bathroom, complete with a bathtub, an indoor shower, and an outdoor shower that cascaded like a waterfall, surrounded by greenery. This, to me, was paradise.

As Sinnu left us with Ifuru's own brand of prosecco and a dinner reservation at the restaurant overlooking the ocean, we were left to explore our new surroundings. First things first, we changed into our bathers, popped the bottle of prosecco, and toasted to a wonderful adventure together.

I'm jealous of myself as I write this. So, to whoever is reading – I'm sorry for gushing, but this was unlike anything I had experienced before. Yes, I've been on nice holidays, but I never got the upgrade or was treated any differently than any other paying customer.

The same could be said for this holiday – the difference was that every single staff member knew our names and treated us like this was our home. And that's exactly how it felt. The staff gave the same treatment to everyone on the island. We were all at home here.

As we stepped into our private pool area, we noticed that beyond the pool, we could walk directly into the ocean from our own garden. This was something else. I can still feel the sand between my toes and the warm waves lapping at my legs. It was the kind of warmth that was so inviting, I literally melted into the sea.

After getting dressed, we wandered around the island to get familiar with our new home. It had everything you could possibly want, but what impressed me the most was the food. Oh my goodness, the food was out of this world.

On our first night, we had dinner at the WaterFront restaurant overlooking the ocean. We sat outside in the moonlight, where we could see fish swimming beneath us. It was unbelievably romantic.

The date of our wedding was Monday, 15 July, just three days after we arrived. We wanted to do it early in the holiday so we could enjoy the honeymoon side of things, and it also freed us up to eat and drink as much as we wanted. If we'd planned the wedding for later in the week, I'm not sure I would have fit into my wedding dress!

I ate so much. The food and drink were endless and all-inclusive. We'd get up reasonably early, hit the breakfast buffet, then have lunch a couple of hours later with a beer or two, followed by afternoon cocktails, beers with pizza from their little beachside pizza hut, and then a lovely dinner in the evening – which always ended with dessert.

If you're on holiday, you *have* to eat the dessert. It's the law! That's something I never used to do. I'd always order whatever I thought was the healthiest thing on the menu and still feel guilty. But here's the strange part: I actually lost some weight while we were away. Maybe it was the hot weather draining my body of all its water weight, or maybe it was the amount of swimming I was doing. According to my Oura ring, I was burning at least 3,000 calories a day. Tom wasn't so lucky – he was fuming when he noticed his lower belly starting to make an appearance by day two.

On the morning of the 15th, we woke up buzzing with excitement. We were set to be married at 4 p.m. at a secret spot at the end of the beach, followed by a couples massage and a romantic dinner on the beach. But then the weather app threw a curveball – a storm was forecast for the exact time of the ceremony.

I panicked. The last thing I wanted was to get married in a tropical storm. I'd dreamt of this moment for at least two weeks, and it had to be perfect. I raised my concerns with Rochelle, and without hesitation, she called Sinnu. Together, they rearranged everything, moving the ceremony up to 2 p.m. so we could enjoy the glorious sunshine.

Feeling relieved, we had a relaxed breakfast, then headed to the pool to chill for a couple of hours before going our separate ways to get ready. All of my belongings were moved to another room so Tom wouldn't see me in my dress before the ceremony. We joked that it would've been a lot easier for *him* to get ready in the other room, with only a shirt and trousers to worry about, while my stuff filled an entire Barbie buggy!

I started getting ready at 1 p.m., thinking it would give me plenty of time. I'd done my own makeup for the last 10 years at *Hollyoaks* and could usually finish in about 20 minutes. I didn't want a makeup artist or someone to do my hair – I'm not big on fuss, and I wanted to look like me.

But somehow, time flew by. I'd barely finished my makeup when I glanced at the clock: it was already 1:40 p.m. I hadn't even touched my hair. Cue panic mode. I got myself in such a flap, trying to tame my wavy bob. Honestly, this was *not* the time for my hair to throw a diva tantrum and start kicking out in all the wrong directions.

Rochelle came to my room to help me into my dress and drive me to the altar. All I could say to her was, 'Crack open the bubbles – I need a drink!' There was also a photographer there, clicking away while I was flapping around.

With a glass of bubbles in one hand and Rochelle doing her best to zip up my dress – it wasn't easy, but thankfully, with the help of the photographer, we managed to fit me into my wedding dress perfectly. Rochelle handed me a bouquet of freshly picked white flowers and asked if I was ready. I knocked back the glass and said, 'Let's go get married.'

The Barbie buggy was waiting for me, and I hopped on the back as it made its way to the other end of the island. As I arrived, I could hear the song I had chosen to walk down the aisle to: 'Love Is a Compass' by Griff. We had chosen that song while driving one day, playing different love songs to see which one fit us – well, *me*. As soon as the opening bars played, goosebumps sprang up all over my body. I turned to Tom and said, 'This is the one.' I'd like to think he felt the same sentiment, but, being a man, if it made me happy, then he was all in.

As I sat on the back of the buggy, I could see Tom waiting for me. At first, he didn't notice I had arrived because the song had been playing on a loop for about 15 minutes (which I didn't find out until later). Traditionally, the song starts playing as the bride is ready to walk down the aisle, signalling her arrival, but that didn't happen.

I started shaking, overwhelmed by the moment, just looking at him and silently saying under my breath, 'Look at me. Look at me, Tom.' Then it happened – he turned around, and our eyes locked. I was flooded with emotion as I wiped a tear away. The song looped back to the beginning, and I walked toward my husband-to-be. He took my hand and told me I looked beautiful.

When we reminisced about that moment later, he said he wouldn't have had it any other way. The surprise of turning around and seeing me in my dress for the first time blew him away. In that moment, everything and everyone else melted away.

What I didn't know was that, while I was getting ready, a huge black cloud had filled the sky, and everyone, including Tom, had been panicking. But as quickly as it came, it disappeared – just long enough for us to say, 'I do.'

Sinnu performed the ceremony, and we exchanged vows in our own words. Tom went first.

'Steph, you have been my confidant, my rock, and my greatest joy. Our friendship has been the foundation of our love, and it is that friendship that makes me certain of the strength of our bond. Today, I promise to always be your best friend and to stand by your side through all the challenges and triumphs that life throws our way. I vow to listen to you, to support you, and to love you unconditionally. Together, we will create a life filled with

adventure, laughter, and love. I am honoured to marry not just the love of my life, but my best friend.'

Then it was my turn.

'Tom, from our first date, I knew there was something extraordinary about you, and you very quickly became my best friend, my confidant, and my greatest love. Today, I stand before you, ready to become your wife, promising to always cherish and respect you. I vow to always support your dreams and to stand by your side through all of life's adventures. I promise to always listen to you, to laugh with you, and to comfort you in times of sorrow. With you, I have found my home and my forever. I love you more than words can express, and I can't wait to spend the rest of my days loving you.'

Saying these words to each other cemented everything we felt. Then came the *I do's* – the first time someone asked me, 'Will you take Tom to be your husband?' It wouldn't be the last.

We sealed our marriage on the island of Ifuru with a kiss, a glass of prosecco, a slice of wedding cake, and a slow dance to Donny Hathaway's 'A Song for You.' A stream of pictures was taken to capture our day, and that was it. It went by so fast.

These special moments in life are meant to be cherished, and I'm holding on to every single frame of that day in my mind.

After the wedding, we went back to our room to call our families, then had a quick change ready for our couples massage. Tom joked that he wasn't sure it was traditional to have another man's hands on his new wife before he did, but I thought it was a wonderful massage. As we were being pampered, we could hear the storm that had been predicted, and we thanked our lucky stars we weren't exchanging vows amidst a hurricane. Because of the bad weather, our wedding meal on the beach was postponed to a clear night later that week. Instead, we were spoiled rotten in our own little dining space at the WaterFront restaurant. The meal and the day were absolute perfection.

Leaving Ifuru was probably one of the hardest challenges we faced as a married couple – at least in the few days we had been wed. For me, staying wasn't a problem; it's not like I had a job to go back to. Unfortunately, Tom did. Like a petulant child, I stuck out my bottom lip, not understanding why Tom couldn't just quit his job so we could stay. Who needs work when you're in paradise? That was my reasoning.

Ifuru will always hold a special place in our hearts, thanks to the people who made our wedding and holiday dreams come true. See you soon, Ifuru.

When we landed back in the UK, it was time for the house renovation reveal and to finally get Tom moved in. Tom swept me off my feet as he opened the front door and carried me over the threshold. Then our jaws dropped. Lisa, my designer, took us on a tour of our new home, and I could not believe the transformation before my eyes. It felt like I was walking into a completely different house. The job Lisa and the boys pulled off while we were away was nothing short of a miracle.

I must admit, though, as beautiful as the house is – and as much as it matched everything I had envisioned for so long – settling in wasn't easy. I was so conscious of everything being new that I treated it like a show home, constantly shouting at the kids to tidy up after themselves. The 'homey' feel was missing. Writing this a few months later, I'm much more settled in.

It was even harder for Tom. He was so used to having his own space, especially with his dogs, Daisy and Lola, who both sadly passed away earlier in the year. Now, he was living with his new wife and two teenage girls. Having separate bedrooms has helped, though. When either of us needs space, we have our own little sanctuaries to retreat to – or, when an argument kicks off, no one has to sleep on the sofa.

Not long after we arrived home, we went full throttle into planning our second wedding, which was set for a month later on the August bank holiday weekend. The first wedding had been so stress-free, I didn't think I'd get away with it again. But to my surprise, planning the wedding at The Coast was just as smooth.

Tom and Blair, the owner, did most of the planning. They'd give me suggestions, and I'd agree. It pretty much went like this:

- **5:00 pm**: Arrival and welcome drinks
- **6:00 pm**: Exchange of vows
- **6:30 pm**: First dance
- **8:30 pm**: Hot and cold food served buffet-style

Throughout the evening, we had the amazing Paul Pashley singing, a saxophonist, and a DJ to take us into the night.

We both wrote guest lists of 30 people each, although it went a little over. The most stressful part? Getting the RSVPs! We knew we'd have a few no-shows – or, in my case, quite a lot – because it was so last minute, and being a bank holiday weekend, many people already had plans.

I am so grateful to everyone who joined us on our special day. Whether they travelled from far away or were people I hadn't seen in a while, their presence meant the world to me.

On the day, I wore a cream-white dress from Reiss. It was beautifully elegant. After an hour, it was time for the vows. My best friend Ross was officiating, and my dad was giving me away. I went upstairs to the office with my two amazing girlfriends, Lisa and Kelly, who helped me into the wedding dress I had worn for the Maldives wedding.

I could hear so much noise downstairs from everyone catching up and enjoying the day. No one seemed to notice when 'Love Is a Compass' started playing – it was my cue to walk down the aisle. I hoped it wouldn't loop endlessly like it did in the Maldives! Thankfully, everyone assumed their positions: family on either side, friends at the back. My two daughters joined me with my dad as I reached the bottom of the stairs. I linked his arm and looked at my daughters, only to see them both in tears.

I relived the moment of the first time we said, 'I do.' As I joined Tom, Ross's celebration of our love was overwhelming, to say the least. All I could do was smile, even as my daughters' sobs grew louder. Then it was time to re-read our vows to each other, and my daughters offered the rings for exchange. I was so happy that my parents and daughters got to share this moment with us – it was perfect.

We said our 'I do's' one last time, sealed it with another kiss, and then took to the dance floor for our first dance. Once again, we chose Donny Hathaway's 'A Song For You', but this time, about a minute into our slow dance – which many thought was choreographed but wasn't – the song effortlessly segued into 'Cuff It' by Beyoncé. That really got the party started as we pulled everyone onto the dance floor. My grandad, however, decided to sit that one out.

The night was a bit of a blur after that – it went by so fast. I barely ate any of the amazing food that had been laid out for us. Instead, I had a permanent glass of LPR wedged in my hand, always topped up. Paul Pashley crooned his way through some classic songs that got everyone dancing, and our DJ smashed out some bangers toward the end of the evening.

It was the best wedding I've ever been to – effortless fun. Everyone told us what an amazing time they had. It was so different, and I got my dream of having my wedding there. It was more than perfect, and I couldn't have asked for more.

Now, let's see what married life brings…. And what the next chapter holds for me.

CHAPTER 18

Breaking My Script,
The Next Chapter

The last few months I have spent reliving some of the worst and the best times of my life: almost dying as a teenager in the pursuit of a pair of legs that could rival Kylie's in those gold hotpants, fulfilling my dreams of becoming an actress, losing myself to my toilet bowl, being so exhausted from chasing butterflies that I would settle for the nearest one that landed in my vicinity, heartbreak, rejection, in love, out of love, to finally meeting the man that I said 'I do' to twice, having my two beautiful daughters, going through early menopause and being axed from the show that started my three-decade career, to now my current situation as a certified life coach.

So what's next? Am I an author? A life coach? Actor? Will I join the millions of people on the podcast bandwagon? Probably, but for now, my new website has been built. Launching my coaching business, which went live on 31st December 2024, is so exciting. Having something of mine that I have created is beyond anything I could have imagined after how my year began. I can't wait to have a front-row seat to watch my clients' transformations. I have also just written my first course, *'The No BS Course to Transforming Your Life in 6 Weeks: Aligning Your Mind, Body, and Purpose'*. I will also be venturing onto the stage at some point and currently have the treatment for a play that is being written for me by my fabulous and talented friend, screen and stage writer Rob Ellis. Theatre is something I have never done professionally before. Comfort zone? This is so far out of mine that it has another postcode. However, I will push myself to do it and embrace the rawness of a live stage show.

Performing live would take me right back to my old Actors Studio roots. Personally and professionally, I think I need it. After being in a soap opera for so many years, I know there are so many layers to delve into—especially now that I have more life experience to draw from. There are endless opportunities to explore, and the possibilities are limitless.

I am sure by now you feel like a passenger in my car – me behind the wheel, navigating you through the journey I have been on so far. Are you wondering if I have conquered my demons? Have I exorcised the monster that ruled my life for decades? Have I really found true love? Or will it only be a matter of time before I become another headline for the *Daily Mail*'s clickbait, feeding the faceless of the comments section who are baying for blood at the mere mention of another failed relationship? Have I really got menopause figured out? Or is it just a matter of time before my body becomes the host to a new influx of symptoms that even hurt won't cure? What kind of life coach will I be when my own mental health has been so fucked up? The learning curve has been real, brutal, and an honesty that I have had to admit to myself and now the world.

So today, as I sit here, pressing play and moving forward, I am no longer drowning or reinforcing bad habits. I am implementing new good habits that align with me. I no longer hold on to the belief that I can't or that I'm not good enough. I only have to look at the evidence of what I have achieved, and that squashes that theory. I am not saying I have it all figured out; sure, I have my days – days when I'd rather shut the world out, lie on my sofa eating Cheetos, and binge the latest Netflix series. And truth be told, yes, I've done that many times. And you know what? It's ok. It's ok to take time out as long as I get back up again.

I even gained a little weight – *shock horror*! This was not easy to do, but it was an important and necessary part of my recovery. After thirty years of being ruled by the notion that being thin is the secret to love and acceptance, I had finally had enough of living in fear. Had it not been for Nick Wall, my nutritionist, I do believe I would still be in the same cycle loop of restriction and guilt. I believe that finally relinquishing control and investing in a professional was the key to freedom of my own mind and breaking the script I had written all those years ago. Having a nutritionist didn't break the bank either. I was so surprised at how affordable he was, just like any coach, whether it be a personal trainer, a life coach or a therapist. I didn't know that Nick would be the person who could help me eat like a normal human being again.

My first meeting with him came about in August 2023 when I was telling my beauty therapist, Alina, all about my keto and fasting lifestyle – trying to convince both her and myself that it's the only diet anyone should be following, especially as a woman for hormone health. Alina listened, and I was waiting for her to agree with everything I was banging on about, but instead, she said, 'You need to get in touch with my nutritionist, Nick Wall. He is amazing, there is no fasting, and you can eat everything, even pizza!' I was dubious and ready to shut her down in my defiance not to cheat on keto, and the thought of anyone else having control over what I put in my mouth shook me to my core—that is, until she promptly whipped out her phone to show me pictures of herself before, then after three months of working with him, sporting what can only be described as washboard abs and thighs to die for.

Wow was the only thought running through my head. And, inputting his number faster than a squirrel on espresso, I called him as soon as I got home to arrange a consultation.

Nick is an award-winning AFN registered nutritionist and a top professional in his field. He offers bespoke nutrition support that is physically and mentally healthy with no silly rules. The following day, I had my first meeting with him, and I told him all about my history and what I was currently doing. I had been messing around over the years with all sorts of fads, from fasting, keto, juicing – you name it. If it promised weight loss, I gave it a go. I was already small, with very little fat to lose, but I had this deep obsession with being as small as possible.

Even though my toxic relationship with Bulimia ended a few years ago, I still used methods of restriction. For instance, I would do the odd 24-hour fast or OMAD (One Meal A Day), as it is referred to in the fasting community, which just made me miserable and starving. I even dabbled with veganism a few years ago, thinking that cutting out any form of meat and dairy would magically get rid of my cellulite, blowing my 'I am doing this for animals' trumpet when, in reality, it was for the elusive thigh gap. (Being a vegan did not magically erase the cottage cheese filter I have going on from behind; it just gave me a bout of acne and anaemia.) With this diagnosis, my next meal was a big, fat, juicy steak. Needless to say, meat has been a huge staple in my diet ever since.

Nick told me to throw any thought of dieting out the window. What he gave me instead was balance – and no restriction. He worked with me on a meal plan where I'd eat six times a day, all whole foods. But if I wanted a snack that came with a label, we could work it in. The gist was carbs and protein or fat and protein for each meal, with vegetables and salad being fair game – eat as much as you want.

He also introduced the concept of a treat meal, not a cheat meal. One night per week, usually Saturday, I could have anything I desired. It was about balance and non-restriction. Well, this blew my mind the thought of allowing myself a pizza with no strings attached, so for my first treat and the first time ever, I ordered a calzone for dinner – and it was bloody delicious.

Exercise was part of the plan, too. I enjoy lifting weights, yoga, walking, and swimming, so shaping up felt effortless. I was never hungry, and I looked forward to my treat every weekend.

When it comes to holidays, Nick says, 'Enjoy the holiday.' Eat and drink as much as you want. It's a small amount of time; you won't pile on the pounds, and when you're back home, you jump straight back on the plan. Holidays are meant to be enjoyed – not spent worrying about your weight. Life is too short. The aim with this plan for me was to eat without the guilt, without having a set of rules. It just so happened that my body started to tighten up, my abs began to shine through, I had boundless energy and, dare I say it, I felt sexy.

I stuck to this plan for around six months. However, it was difficult when the extension was being built, as I had no kitchen to make elaborate meals from scratch. I became lazy, lost my rhythm, and fell back into old patterns.

Once again, I began to restrict myself, and those old feelings started to wash over me—guilt creeping in whenever I treated myself. Part of me was still hanging on to something; I would still scrutinise myself and make sure I got [X] amount of exercise done if I had what was deemed a 'naughty' food.

I faced my fear head-on, throwing myself into a territory that goes against everything I have done so far – I purposely gained weight, a few pounds, just to see how much I would have to eat to do it. I knew I could lose it again, so what was the harm? I was so sick and tired of fearing my trigger foods I needed to do something drastic to turn them into just foods. I wanted to permanently remove the anxiety over having a biscuit or the guilt of having a pizza once in a while and to choose the meal I really wanted to eat in restaurants instead of scouring for the healthiest, most unappetising dish on the menu and saying I was full when I really wanted the sticky toffee pudding for dessert. The amount of times I have said that I didn't like cheese so I wouldn't look out of place refusing a slice of pizza when it was offered to me in a group setting. Who the hell does not like cheese? It is the HOLY GRAIL of foods. I really do feel for my lactose-intolerant friends.

So although I felt that last year I was finally breaking free of all my restrictions, especially with the help of Nick, now purposefully eating all the foods I once would find myself seeing the contents in reverse into my toilet, not only did I ALLOW myself, now this is so important, by allowing it, my brain just went, OK, like it was shrugging its shoulders at me wondering why I hadn't done this years ago.

The most amazing thing is that for someone who used to have a panic attack at the thought of eating anything 'naughty', it feels amazing to finally let go of the control I held over myself for most of my life. I am not here advocating an all-you-can-eat junk food buffet lifestyle, far from it. I am advocating for balance, no extremes, no fad diets, no restriction, no cutting carbs, and no fasting. When you have had an eating disorder, fasting is just another form of restriction, no matter how good the benefits are.

When I decided to say *'fuck it'* and eat the 'More to Share' bag of Maltesers for the third night in a row, say yes to the seventh Deliveroo meal of convenience, and not move from my sofa because it was December – the month I affectionately call *'the fuck-it month'* – I said to myself, *Let's see what happens.*

Truth is, I did not blow up like a balloon the next day or the day after that. But as the new year approached, my clothes felt a little snug, my face a little rounder, and all I could say to myself was, *Don't look at yourself naked in the mirror* in fear that I might actually leave my house and Forrest Gump my way around the UK until all traces of December had been erased from my body. I had put on weight, but it took a whole month of anything I desired to put on a few pounds – not days or even a week.

Feeling these new curves isn't as scary as I thought it would be and my husband loves them and tells me how beautiful I am even when I don't believe it or him. I am not in the best shape of my life and, I'm not going to lie, I did freak out a little bit, thinking, *What the hell have I done?"* But I told myself over and over that it was ok. I know that going back to my plan with Nick and getting back into my fitness routine will shed those extra pounds, however long it takes. I will then work with Nick on maintenance and mentality, keeping the balance right for life.

The most amazing gift to come out of this is I no longer crave processed junk food, I no longer feel triggered, and I no longer feel guilt. I now know that I can have a treat once in a while. I know that I can go on holiday and enjoy everything on offer, knowing that it is just a moment in time. Life is for living, not for saying no to things that give us pleasure, and not to be ruled by what other people think of you and your body.

When I put things into perspective and created some boundaries, everything started to feel a lot lighter. It now feels easier to show up for myself. I realised that I am the only person responsible for making my life the happiest it can be. I'm the only one who can reach my goals. I'm the only one who can take care of my body. I'm the only one who can make my money.

I don't have someone calling me every day with a call time anymore, so it's up to me to get myself out of bed and show up. I am the CEO of my own life. So now, with my new business, being a life coach is just another string to the bow of what I can do. I would love to explore the opportunity to step into another character's world and write another book

– all the while showing up where I am needed most: as a mother and a wife.

Letting go of what went before, embracing the road ahead, and learning from every challenge and obstacle I face. We are not promised forever, but we live like we are. I know that for most of my life, I have taken my health for granted, treating my body like a garbage can, thinking that there won't be repercussions. But there are, and as I get older, my health is now my number one priority – it has to be.

If you are reading this and have survived an eating disorder, or you are firmly in the grips of this awful disease, or you know someone who is and has no idea what to do, please do not lose hope. I am a survivor, but it took me thirty years. I wish I knew then what I know now and stopped wasting so much time. I can't claw back those years of disordered thinking. I can only move forward and remind myself every day that I am beautiful, no matter my shape.

Social media has caused—and continues to cause—significant damage to children, teenagers, and young adults by promoting a false narrative of perfection. Body shaming has always been prevalent and considered fair game, but now, more than ever, it is crucial that we stand in our own power and refuse to accept the scrutiny of others.

I need to set an example for my girls, and I hope they see what I am doing for myself now. I also hope that I have inspired them to love themselves, place themselves on their own pedestal, embrace the bodies they are in, and pursue any dream they desire.

Well, within reason… I can't see either of them flying to the moon any time soon or performing open-heart surgery one day. But I truly hope they recognise themselves as the wonderful, beautiful beings they are and never let anyone make them feel less than that.

My husband, Tom? This man has been through the wringer with me, and he is still my number one supporter. He has stuck by me when the shit hit the fan, loving me when I lost myself in my own crazy, offering to watch documentaries about menopause just so he could understand what I was going through and who he needed to be for me.

The last four years have been a rollercoaster. Before him, I would have run away amidst the tough conversations and the loss of communication, but I see past all of that, knowing that neither of us was going anywhere – coming back to the table again and again, listening and honouring what each other needed in the moment. Tom, you are my best friend, and I am so excited to build a marriage with you.

To the fans of *Hollyoaks* who have watched me grow up on your TV and those of you who loved to hate Cindy, thank you from the bottom of my heart for your support and dedication for all of these years. *Hollyoaks* will always have a special place in my heart, and I will never forget the friendships, the laughs, the breakdowns, the gossip and most of all, Cindy. I miss you the most. I will see you all soon, whether it be on the screen, on stage or listening to me ranting on a podcast on your morning commute.

To all the people who have been a part of my journey—the ones who have left, the ones who have stayed, the ones who are all in, and the ones who are just testing the water – whether you are here with me for a reason, a season, or a lifetime…

To all the exes, the dates, the long-terms, the 'I can't believe I did that' moments. The walks of shame. The heartbreakers and the ones who truly loved me. You all taught me something – the good and the bad. There may have been a few wrong turns, but those turns led me to Tom.

To my menopause warriors out there: every second person in the world will go through this change. We need to make our voices louder. We need to be heard. We need to pave the way for our daughters and their daughters after them. We've got this.

The second half may not be a picnic so far, and you may feel like you've been thrown into a permanent heatwave with no air conditioning, but you *will* get your second spring. So, don't be too hard on yourself, and look after that amazing body of yours.

Now, it is time to move on to the next chapter. I will continue to learn, grow, and be my own cheerleader. I will face life's challenges head-on instead of living in fear and staying in my comfort zone. I will love and accept myself for who I am, break the script of the pages of my life I had written, and finally own every last choice, decision, and lesson.

It's time to write a new book, one page at a time.

THANK YOU FOR READING MY BOOK!

Just to say thanks — if you'd like to work with me,
don't hesitate to contact me.

I appreciate your interest in my book and value your feedback as it helps me improve future versions of this book. I would appreciate it if you could leave your invaluable review on Amazon.com with your feedback. Thank you!